More From the American Aca

**For additional parenting resources, visit the HealthyChildren bookstore at
https://shop.aap.org/for-parents.**

*This book is also available in Spanish.

High Five Discipline

Positive Parenting for Happy, Healthy, Well-Behaved Kids

Candice W. Jones, MD, FAAP

American Academy of Pediatrics
DEDICATED TO THE HEALTH OF ALL CHILDREN®

American Academy of Pediatrics Publishing Staff
Mary Lou White, *Chief Product and Services Officer/SVP, Membership, Marketing, and Publishing*
Mark Grimes, *Vice President, Publishing*
Holly Kaminski, *Editor, Consumer Publishing*
Shannan Martin, *Production Manager, Consumer Publications*
Amanda Helmholz, *Medical Copy Editor*
Sara Hoerdeman, *Marketing Manager, Consumer Products*

Published by the American Academy of Pediatrics
345 Park Blvd
Itasca, IL 60143
Telephone: 630/626-6000
Facsimile: 847/434-8000
www.aap.org

The American Academy of Pediatrics is an organization of 67,000 primary care pediatricians, pediatric medical subspecialists, and pediatric surgical specialists dedicated to the health, safety, and well-being of all infants, children, adolescents, and young adults.

The information contained in this publication should not be used as a substitute for the medical care and advice of your pediatrician. There may be variations in treatment that your pediatrician may recommend based on individual facts and circumstances.

Statements and opinions expressed are those of the author and not necessarily those of the American Academy of Pediatrics.

Any websites, brand names, products, or manufacturers are mentioned for informational and identification purposes only and do not imply an endorsement by the American Academy of Pediatrics (AAP). The AAP is not responsible for the content of external resources. Information was current at the time of publication.

The publishers have made every effort to trace the copyright holders for borrowed materials. If they have inadvertently overlooked any, they will be pleased to make the necessary arrangements at the first opportunity.

This publication has been developed by the American Academy of Pediatrics. The contributors are expert authorities in the field of pediatrics. No commercial involvement of any kind has been solicited or accepted in the development of the content of this publication. Disclosures: The author reports no disclosures.

Every effort is made to keep *High Five Discipline: Positive Parenting for Happy, Healthy, Well-Behaved Kids* consistent with the most recent advice and information available from the American Academy of Pediatrics.

Special discounts are available for bulk purchases of this publication. Email Special Sales at nationalaccounts@aap.org for more information.

Printed in the United States of America

9-469/0921   1 2 3 4 5 6 7 8 9 10
CB0126
ISBN: 978-1-61002-517-1
eBook: 978-1-61002-520-1
EPUB: 978-1-61002-518-8
Kindle: 978-1-61002-519-5

Cover design by Daniel Rembert
Publication design by Rattray Design

Library of Congress Control Number: 2020948353

What People Are Saying

In *High Five Discipline,* mom and pediatrician Dr Candice Jones coaches parents and caregivers on how to motivate, shape, and encourage their kids into appropriately behaving. Her must-read positive parenting guide offers tips and tricks for each stage of a child's development to help every family move beyond tantrums and squabbles to high fives and hugs!

> —Tanya Altmann, MD, FAAP, founder of Calabasas Pediatrics, editor in chief of *Caring for Your Baby and Young Child*

Personally, I think discipline is the hardest part of parenting. As parents, we imagine we need to "make" our kids behave, "win" battles of will, and "enforce" our rules. In fact, good discipline involves teaching, positive reinforcement, and, as Dr Candice Jones points out in her new book, *High Five Discipline,* loving our children in the most active sense of the word. Rather than speaking as an expert from on high, Dr Jones shares her own struggles as a parent, including the story of how she came to discipline her own children differently than she was disciplined as a child. She lays out in clear, easy-to-follow steps how parents can reframe discipline from an exhausting constant fight for control into a loving collaboration between parent and child that leads children to grow into their best selves. I can just hear Dr Jones' voice as I read this book, and it just makes me smile. Once you start reading, you will too!

> —David L. Hill, MD, FAAP, coauthor of *Co-parenting Through Separation and Divorce*

Dr Candice applies PEACE to share her heart, expertise, and practical wisdom on positive parenting for children. Drawing from her own powerful story, she warmly guides parents through an often fraught, but critical, element of raising healthy, well-adjusted children in a way that sets everyone up for long-term success, including ensuring that parents are mindful of their own triggers and need to breathe!

> —Nusheen Ameenuddin, MD, MPH, MPA, FAAP, Mayo Clinic Children's Center, chair of Diversity and Inclusion of the Mayo Clinic Health System, chair of the American Academy of Pediatrics Council on Communications and Media

As a licensed mental health therapist who specializes in play therapy, I am pleased to share that this book by far will be one of my greatest resources to use with the families that I serve. Dr Jones gives examples that help you to recognize your own parenting style and that also help you to apply some of the strategies and techniques shared in this much-needed book. Whether you are a parent or work with youth, you will find the practical strategies in this book insightful.

—Shanta Barton-Stubbs, LMHC, ThD, founder of New Image Youth Center, author of *There Is Good in My Hood*

I'm so proud of Dr Candice Jones' (MSM class of 2006) achievement in developing the definitive guide on parenting discipline. Endorsed by the American Academy of Pediatrics, Dr Jones' book teaches us that physical punishment should never be part of discipline for parents; there are better, evidence-based methods.

—David A. Levine, MD, FAAP, professor of pediatrics and clerkship director, Morehouse School of Medicine

Dr Candice's personal and professional perspectives in *High Five Discipline* are a must-read for any adult caring for a child. It is an easy read with such a helpful guide for disciplining and loving children so they can be successful adults. Thank you for giving a voice to this important topic.

—Joelle Simpson, MD, MPH, FAAP

High Five Discipline is a rich, comprehensive blend of the pragmatic rooted in evidence-informed guidance on 21st century parenting. It is well organized with strategically placed callout boxes that allow the reader to utilize the book as a valuable at-their-fingertips tool. The Adult in the Mirror part on parental self-care is especially compelling. Congratulations to Dr Candice Jones on this wonderful contribution to the AAP pool of parent resources.

—Joseph L. Wright, MD, MPH, FAAP, member of the American Academy of Pediatrics Board Committee on Equity, professor of pediatrics and health policy at the University of Maryland schools of Medicine and Public Health

In her book, *High Five Discipline,* Dr Candice Jones gives parents and caregivers a practical and positive guide to understanding and disciplining their children. Through clear and relatable examples, Dr Candice shows us how to provide loving discipline, intentionally and consistently, for our children, which is the key not only to improving a child's behavior but to ensuring her healthy development so that she can thrive in school and in life. This book is a must-read not only for parents but for grandparents, aunts and uncles, teachers, doctors, and community leaders because we all have a stake in the healthy development of our children.

—Leslie Hartog, chief strategy officer, the K-Ready Community Project

Dr Jones is spot on. Behavior is the language of children. We adults are responsible for interpreting and responding in a way that positively guides a child and strengthens the bond. I highly recommend this easy read, which is packed full of practical advice.

—Karen Willis, CWDP, BA, MPA, chief executive officer, Early
        Learning Coalition of Orange County

While I am not a parent, I have worked with children of all ages throughout my career. In this aspect, Dr Candice Jones' book has been influential in how my organization helps and fights for at-risk youth every day. As we prepare to launch our first-ever school, I am asking all educators to adopt the High Five Essentials of Effective and Positive Parenting as a way to further their professional and personal development with real-life scenarios from a leading expert.

—Glenton Gilzean Jr, president and CEO, Central Florida Urban League

To parents and other caregivers trying to figure out the best way to discipline their children, I sincerely hope *High Five Discipline* helps you solve your discipline puzzle and create a positive family discipline plan.

To my family, sanctuary for me is at home with you: the best dad and husband ever, Derrick, and the 2 greatest accomplishments and responsibilities of my life, Miles and Marlee!

Candice W. Jones, MD, FAAP

Equity, Diversity, and Inclusion Statement

The American Academy of Pediatrics is committed to principles of equity, diversity, and inclusion in its publishing program. Editorial boards, author selections, and author transitions (publication succession plans) are designed to include diverse voices that reflect society as a whole. Editor and author teams are encouraged to actively seek out diverse authors and reviewers at all stages of the editorial process. Publishing staff are committed to promoting equity, diversity, and inclusion in all aspects of publication writing, review, and production.

Contents

Part 1

Personal History: My "Her"story

Part 2

Essential Discipline Dynamics

Part 3

Adult in the Mirror

Part 4

Child Basics: Act Like a Parent but Think Like a Child

Part 5

Establishing a Family Discipline Plan

Acknowledgments

Writing *High Five Discipline* has been a journey and a labor of love. Without Michelle Kelly, the early drafts and the foundation of this finished product would not be possible. You walked me through the technicalities of the writing process and provided the checks and balances for engaging content. Thank you, Michelle, for your contribution.

Thank you, AAP Publishing, for taking this book to the next level and bringing it to a world-renowned platform. A special shout-out to Tanya Altmann, MD, FAAP, for introducing me to you. Barrett, Holly, Sara, Amanda, and Shannan, thank you for supporting me every step of the way. It has been an absolute pleasure working with you. Teamwork makes the dream work!

I'm so grateful for "my village": my great-grandparents, Herbert and Madeline Wiggins; grandparents, Clarissa Young and Frankie Watters; parents, Sandra and Charlie Gilbert as well as Louis Watters Jr; parents-in-law, Andrew and Annie Walker; and siblings, aunts/uncles, cousins, teachers/professors/attendings, mentors, and friends—both past and present—for contributing to the person I am today and supporting me wholeheartedly in so many ways that I can't name them all.

Thank you, Edgewater Pediatrics. To my boss and colleague, Ted Kaplan, and my office manager/nurse/best friend, Elisabeth Kaplan, I appreciate our family and work environment and your support of my professional development outside the clinic—my community work, podcast, book, media, etc.

To the parents/caregivers and children I am honored to serve, thank you for allowing me to be the "auntie" in your family and for trusting me enough to listen. You teach me more than you know.

To the other members of my cabinet, Lauren Parker, Tina Morgan, Teresa Carter, and Stephanie Pennington, I truly appreciate your taking the time to read early drafts of this book, offer thoughtful suggestions, and support me in other ways personally and professionally.

While writing this book, I stood on the shoulders of giants in the field of pediatrics, child behavior, development, and parenting. I'm grateful to all the experts whose work informed this book. Thank you to the reviewers who took time out of their busy schedules to peer-review this book. A special thanks to Adiaha Spinks-Franklin, MD, MPH, FAAP; Kenneth R. Ginsburg, MD, MS Ed, FAAP; and Arthur Lavin, MD, FAAP. Because of you, I am confident this book is tried and true. I also appreciate the following American Academy of Pediatrics groups for their review of this book:

- Committee on Psychosocial Aspects of Child and Family Health
- Council on Child Abuse and Neglect
- Section on Developmental and Behavioral Pediatrics

Finally, to my dear husband and children, Derrick, Miles, and Marlee, thank you so much for being understanding throughout this project. Sorry I missed cooking some meals, going on a few outings, and cuddling up for family movie nights because I needed to write. I'm all yours now! I'm filled with gratitude that you allowed me to share our challenges and successes on these pages to show families they are not alone and they can overcome together. In so many ways, writing this book has helped me become a better parent—a positive guide for you, Miles and Marlee, through this thing called life. Your dad and I look forward to watching you both soar on your own . . . we love you unconditionally.

Introduction

A parent using positive parenting skills is a sight to see! A "boss" mom or dad or other caregiver who knows how to maneuver their kids skillfully through any situation. Cool. Calm. Collected. This mom uses a sweet and nurturing, yet firm voice. Her children choose to follow or learn to follow, because she's loving, full of praise, patient, and speaking their language. Putting a smile on her face or getting a high five from her is all the reward they need.

Somehow she has superpowers—Spidey senses, on high alert, to foresee and anticipate her child's next move and get around it. Yes, she is a master re-director, because she knows that being proactive sets her children up for success and keeps her from having to figure out a consequence for their misbehaving. She is working smarter, not harder. Even though this mom may have been raised "old school," she realizes that the discipline her children need to develop well and flourish in life does not have to be physical or unkind.

You love when she says, "Nice hands," "Is that a good choice?" or "Let's go this way," as she heads down the supermarket aisle, knowing her child will eventually follow. She carefully chooses her words and actions, knowing they can hurt and scar for life.

And when her toddler throws a tantrum in the middle of the supermarket, she keeps shopping, as if nothing were happening, while others look on, waiting for her reaction. To their surprise, she gives attention to and praises her child for calming down. You realize her focus is not to punish but to teach, guide, and model appropriate behavior. Now that's what you call *positive parenting*!

In the moment, this mom may feel frustrated, embarrassed, and judged, but she sticks to the skills that she believes work and positively influence her child's growth and development. Spanking and yelling are out of the question because she knows that she can discipline her child without hitting.

Others may question whether this mom maintains composure this well at home. But consider, she has taken some parenting classes, or read several parenting books, or maybe had formal education in child behavior. She knows that parenting this way—peacefully, positively, and proactively—doesn't come naturally. It takes hard work and dedication. And yes, you, too, can parent with positive parenting skills and raise happy, healthy, well-behaved children.

Hands down, parenting is the hardest yet most rewarding job on the planet! The experience can take you on a roller coaster of emotions, from anger to joy, all in the same day. Parenting journeys can also be very different. Some parents are anxious, first-time moms and dads hovering over their bundle of joy to make sure all is well. Other parents have graduated the newbie phase and are now managing 3 or 4 children's behavior. Through these unique experiences, parents vary in attitudes and beliefs toward parenting. Some believe in being strict with their kids, whereas others foster a more democratic approach. And even within families, each child often requires different parenting strategies—what works for one child may not work for another. You may feel you've done a great job with your first child because they listen and follow instructions with ease. Then the next one rebels at every turn, leaving you wondering, "What am I doing wrong with this child, and how do I handle this?" There's so much to navigate in parenthood. But don't worry, I am here to help you create the best path for your parenting journey.

Even though parenting styles may differ, all parents share a common goal of wanting to raise great kids who become caring, successful, and productive adults. Our kids are the future. Our job is to do the best we can to help make their future as bright as possible. Discipline is an important part of parenting that does the "shaping."

The way we discipline our children not only shapes their behavior but affects their health and overall well-being. There is no shortage of advice on the right and wrong ways to discipline children. Just chat with Grandma or read a mommy blog. Unfortunately, not all advice is correct, and some can harm children. So you're on the right track by reading this book—backed by the science of child development and behavior—to improve your discipline skills as a parent and to improve your child's behavior. Study after study has shown that improvement in various parenting skills greatly enhances the social, cognitive, and behavioral development of a child. And the evidence is clear that aversive disciplinary tactics, such as hitting, yelling, and shaming, have negative outcomes on physical, mental, and social-emotional health.

As a pediatrician, I counsel hundreds of parents each year about how to discipline effectively and manage common behavior problems in their children. In every case, I encourage parents to use positive parenting. This approach highlights what I call the High Five Essentials: Knowledge of Child Development and Parenting Skills, Good Relational Health Between Parent and Child, Encouraging Positive Behavior, Discouraging and Correcting Negative Behavior, and Managing the Environment. All are essential pieces to the discipline puzzle.

Imagine bringing home the world's largest jigsaw puzzle, with thousands of pieces! Skilled puzzle builders recommend that you follow the big picture on the box for guidance, which represents monitoring the ever-changing life of your child. Next, you should sort the pieces by colors symbolizing the ages, stages, and developmental phases your family will experience together. Then, a good strategy is to start at the simplest point and begin building from there. Some parts of the puzzle may be particularly challenging, just as they will be with managing your kids' behavior. But stay calm, take breaks, and keep working at the puzzle. The pride and joy you feel when you connect all the puzzle pieces together will be well worth the effort.

High Five Discipline will help you put all the pieces of effective and positive parenting together to create a family discipline plan that both promotes appropriate behavior and limits problem behavior in your home. Happy, healthy, well-behaved kids in the making!

About This Book

igh Five Discipline helps parents and other child caregivers create a discipline plan that promotes appropriate behavior and limits problem behavior. It shows parents how to piece together the best concepts and strategies of discipline in a more positive, nonphysical, and peaceful way to not only guide child behavior but also support overall health and development.

Because peace is at the core of what parents hope to achieve in family life, each part of this book represents a letter in the word *peace*.

Part 1
Personal History: My "Her"story

As a pediatrician, I am most impactful with patients and families when I am open and honest about my personal experiences and challenges as a parent. For this reason, Part 1, my "her"story (aha moment), gives insight into my life: how I was raised, my parenting journey, and how I use what I know as a pediatrician to effectively work with kids. I hope this will help you remember that I'm not judging. I'm just sharing what's best. I hope this will also encourage you to explore your story because our past can positively guide the way we discipline.

Part 2
Essential Discipline Dynamics

Part 2 is all about, you guessed it, discipline. It's time for many parents to remodel the way they discipline because the old-school approach doesn't work and harms children. This part explains the need for discipline, explains what discipline should be, and offers a positive and effective model for anyone caring for children.

Part 3

Adult in the Mirror

Part 3 focuses on parents or any person who touches the life of a child, including family members, teachers, and babysitters. This part discusses how self-reflection and self-care are important in becoming the best parent possible. It also highlights other key elements of parenting, such as modeling and managing expectations. And finally, you will learn mindfulness strategies and other coping skills that are necessary to peacefully handle the many frustrations that come with parenting.

Part 4

Child Basics: Act Like a Parent but Think Like a Child

Part 4 shows parents how to view things from a child's perspective. It focuses on understanding why children do what they do at various developmental stages in childhood. It also shares age-based strategies that promote positive behavior. Finally, it raises awareness about the health impacts of adverse childhood experiences, which can happen with negative discipline.

Part 5

Establishing a Family Discipline Plan

Got skills? If you think you're up for the challenge, take these interactive tests to find out! They recreate the most common behavior challenges with kids, such as tantrums, hitting, sibling rivalry, and disobedience. A way for you to lather, rinse, repeat. Then you're ready to piece together your family discipline plan. To support your efforts, I provide a template and a sample.

Before we start, I'd like for you to recite the following parent/caregiver pledge. As you strive to improve along this discipline journey, this pledge will remind you to relax, relate, and release to keep the peace!

Parent/Caregiver Pledge: I pledge to quit spanking, yelling, shaming, or taking any action that can damage my child. I pledge to listen more, think before I respond, and act in love, not anger.

Please note, names and certain specifics used throughout this book have been changed to maintain confidentiality.

PART 1

Personal History: My "Her"story

When you stand and share your story in an empowering way, your story will heal you and your story will heal somebody else.

—Iyanla Vanzant

Hi there! Allow me to reintroduce myself. I'm Candice Jones, MD, FAAP, but you can call me Dr Candice. I'm a board-certified pediatrician, a wife, and a mother of 2 beautiful children. I want to share with you my journey to becoming the parent I am today, or tomorrow, because I work hard every day to get better at parenting my kids. In addition, I hope to encourage you to explore your story because our past can positively guide the way we discipline.

Well, to put it mildly, I was raised "old school." I was spanked probably 10 times a day on a "good" day. And yes, I was left with some marks that would qualify as abuse nowadays. But in the '70s and '80s, spanking was the norm; I even got a couple of paddlings from my teachers.

My mom was a teenager when she became a parent. She had inadequate parenting and coping skills and an immature brain of her own. She was stressed-out from a bad marriage and trying her best to make ends meet. She had little time for "children's mess" and was irritable, impatient, and quick to grab whatever to "straighten you out." She did the best she could to care for us. I know that, and I love her for it.

I remember, late one Christmas Eve, like most nights, I wet the bed. My older sister tattled on me. My mom spanked me as usual, shouting about how tired she was of my bedwetting, how I was just too "lazy" to get up and go to the bathroom, and how Santa Claus was going to "catch me out of bed and put ashes in my eyes."

Time out!

No child wants to lie in a wet bed or pees in their bed on purpose. Bedwetting is typically a normal, common, and involuntary phase outgrown in young childhood. Concerns should be discussed with your pediatrician, not through punishing your child.

She ordered me to take a bath as she went back to bed. I was terrified and bathed so quickly that I used only a cup of water that night. Thank God Santa never showed up!

And the list goes on and on: The vice grip pinches in the grocery store that brought me to my knees and the look that dared me to cry aloud. Being sent to get the belt or picking the switch from a tree for my spanking. The threats and the words that cut like knives. And believing that I had caused my mother's wrath and that she was supposed to act this way. "My fault. Look what I made her do," I thought.

I hear people from all walks of life say things like "I deserved those whuppings, I was bad" or "That's what's wrong with kids these days, parents can't discipline (spank) them anymore." Sadly, these learned behaviors, attitudes, and beliefs toward parenting and children felt normal to me as well. Children are indoctrinated into abuse—verbal, physical, and mental—generation after generation in many households.

And you may be thinking, "You're a doctor and you turned out great, even though your mother spanked you!" Yes, I turned out "great," not because of what my mom did wrong but because of what she did right. And it's perfectly OK to acknowledge having both kinds of experiences.

My mom was the best cook. I can feel my mouth watering right now, just thinking about the meals she prepared for us! She taught us to believe in God and took us to church regularly, where we were guided, nurtured, and supported. She demonstrated hard work and self-determination by caring for us while she was going to school to become a nurse. And she knew how to gather support from "the village." Our grandparents and great-grandparents were within walking distance and gave us all the hugs, kisses, and treats that a child could ever want. That's just part of the reason I turned out great.

On the other hand, I carry some baggage from the adults in my life doing some things wrong. Therefore, I internalized what I saw and heard and grew up aggressive, impatient, and blaming of others for my actions and harsh words. I also developed an intolerance for children. I would say, "He's bad," "She needs her behind whipped," or "They're so spoiled, because their momma doesn't spank them." (Not the makings of a pediatrician, I know.) I definitely embraced this philosophy at one time. But not anymore!

What changed my mind, you ask? Well, the phenomenal poet Maya Angelou said it best: "Do the best you can until you know better. Then when you know better, you do better." I've witnessed teachers, parents, and other caregivers disciplining differently—with a more positive and peaceful approach—and the kids turned out amazing; they were happier and calmer even. Also, 15 years of pediatric practice taught me better ways to relate to kids and a handful of strategies to encourage them to behave without all the drama.

Children misbehave. Children need discipline. And children who don't have it tend to go astray. But it's also true that discipline doesn't have to be strict, harsh, or aggressive. Appropriate discipline should be administered with love and a spirit of training or teaching, all to foster the greatest potential in our children. And since I've had children of my own, I've put these strategies to the test. This is where the rubber meets the road!

During my son's preschool years, he got into trouble a lot for tantrums—loud crying, kicking his shoes off, falling to the floor, and even running away. He was in a traditional, private school setting that worked well with "in-the-box" kids but not those whose behavior posed a challenge. I was working full-time then—about 30 minutes outside of town. The school would call me and request that I come get him. I'd say, "Wait . . . what? . . . but I'm seeing patients and sick kids at that, who need me to be here. You can't handle one crying kid?" I'd hear, "Sorry, you have to come get him." And on the days he stayed, I still received messages and emails, and ultimately attended several meetings "to fix this," but oddly, they offered no solutions.

When I asked his preschool teacher to implement a classroom behavior plan, which included praise for appropriate behavior, she reportedly felt it would be unfair to the other kids. His next teacher called him "violent," obviously not knowing the definition, and took pictures of him crying and hanging upside down from his chair, as if I didn't see these things at home (he was the same everywhere—there was no turning this behavior on and off). Another teacher called him "bad." One principal suggested that he would grow up with an anger problem, and another one lied to cover their blunders, blaming a 4-year-old for "crying his way out of his problems." Needless to say, I took him out midyear and received a refund after exposing their inadequacies. Teachers and principals need positive parenting skills too!

What I regret most is how I reacted toward my son and his unwanted behaviors. I let the pressure from the school, my own frustrations, and others' judgments and advice influence me. I went into fix-it mode, briefly reverting to old-school parenting to force him to behave. I even hired an unlicensed boot camp–style, so-called, behavior therapist. My temperament and old belief system of control played into interactions with my son. I would sometimes yell, lose my cool, and say things out of anger and frustration that I later regretted.

Now, however, I know those things are damaging and counterproductive and didn't help him settle down, manage his emotions, or make better choices. They actually made his behavior worse. So I prayed and found that the answer was—and always will be—love. I'm not talking about the deep, emotional love that we feel for our children but the verb *love,* the act of love. How we love. Did my son feel loved when I screamed at him, spanked him, or put him down? No. Would he model my behaviors and aggression? Yes, and he was doing just that!

It was clear that I should act more lovingly, compassionately, and empathically. My responses needed to be kind, patient, and understanding. I had to focus on teaching, guiding, and nurturing him. I also had to shift my attention from fixing my son to examining myself. I needed to relax, think clearly, and define who I wanted and needed to be for my child in those tense moments. All adults need to do this if they choose to have or work with children.

One thing is for sure: it's easier to react. Parenting well is hard work. Whew! Going from angry to calm, negative to positive, impatient to patient, blaming to understanding, and reactionary to proactive takes a lot of effort, but the reward and positive results you witness will be worth it.

Despite popular belief, my son wasn't being defiant and trying to make my life miserable; he was just a child behaving innocently and immaturely, with self-driven wants and poor emotional control. He needed nurturing, guidance, and consistent, positive parenting.

So I went part-time and homeschooled him for about 8 months before finding a school that was a good fit for him—fit is key. He was fully evaluated, which highlighted areas requiring medical attention and explained his behaviors and social-emotional difficulties. We got help from a few great, highly skilled professionals, and I took a parenting class. Yes, I, the pediatrician, did!

I learned and improved my parenting skills. I began to pay attention when he behaved well and taught him better when he misbehaved, over and over again. I purposefully tried to find the positive in every situation and gave him the benefit of the doubt. I learned his triggers, what encouraged him to make positive choices, and what made him shut down or not adhere. Then I worked to anticipate his actions and made adjustments for more positive outcomes. Miraculously, I began to see his behavior improve as I began to praise him with a thumbs-up, pat on the back, or high five. And he even began to express disappointment over things he did wrong and make better choices.

I know you may be unable to do exactly what I did, because we don't all have the same resources. But you need to know when to seek help and when old-fashioned tactics just won't do. That's why I've written this book. To share with you all the strategies I've learned along the way and to offer guidance on how you can reclaim a joyous family (home) life.

The icing on the cake was finding a wonderful Montessori school that focused on educating the "whole" child and believed in individualized education. Academics are important, but meeting the social-emotional and developmental needs of students is just as important. My son can lie or sit quietly on the floor or at a desk in his classroom. He has a place to go, to "chill out," when his emotions are getting the best of him, and other classroom strategies promote his educational success. He has Peace Class and Life Lab. He receives gifted instruction with internships to stimulate and hone his exceptional mind. And most importantly, his teachers *believe* that he is loving, kind, and trying very hard to make positive choices every day. Therefore, he has matured beautifully and we see a bright future. Woo-hoo!

Many parents share similar challenges with me in and out of the clinic. I always tell my story to give support and hope. I encourage them to do what I did myself.

- Calm down and do *your* work.
- Get help and improve your skills.
- Focus on the positive.
- Act with love.
- Meet the child where they are.
- Teach with patience.
- Teach them better choices.
- Plan for family success.

Parenting and working with children are 2 of the most difficult jobs. There are no perfect parents. Just those of us who strive to do better. Start where you are, and keep working at it. Your child will thank you and love you for it. Their happiness, health, and well-being depend on it. If I can do it, so can you!

PART 2

Essential Discipline Dynamics

It is easier to build strong children than to repair broken men.

—FREDERICK DOUGLAS

Chapter 1

Discipline Basics: The What, Why, and How

As I paused outside my patients' room to send out a quick prescription, I heard a pop-like noise and Mr Allen yelling, "Give it to her! Share with your sister!" I entered the room to find Destiny crying in the corner and little Dana playing with a toy. "What's going on?" I inquired. Mrs Allen explained that Destiny was in trouble, because she wouldn't share with her sister. After exchanging pleasantries, I attempted to bring the 2 girls together for a little playtime to demonstrate sharing, but Dad interjected and said, "You sit right where I told you, Destiny! She's gonna do what I say, Doc." I reassured Dad that I was just trying to help as their pediatrician. Then I discussed how sharing is challenging for toddlers and tried to encourage the Allens to show their girls how to share and be patient as they master these skills over time. Furthermore, forcing Destiny to share didn't equip her to share independently. "Refusing to share is not that serious," I joked. "Teaching her to share is all the discipline you need here, not spanking or time-out." I hoped the message hit home for their family's sake.

It turns out, the Allens aren't the only parents who believe discipline requires harsh or strict parenting. Misconceptions about discipline hinder us from guiding our children more positively and effectively. In this chapter, I tackle some of the common myths about discipline to clear up any misconceptions and to get us all on the same page and head us down the right discipline path.

What Is Discipline?

The word *discipline* originates from the Latin words *discipulus*, meaning "pupil," and *disciplinare*, meaning "to teach." So in its simplest form, discipline means to teach. Parents are the teachers and children are the pupils. Parents, think back to when you were younger in school. Who was your favorite teacher—the teacher, the mentor, or even the coach who positively influenced your life? Do you remember? I'm sure we can all agree this person could be best described as patient, kind, understanding, positive, fun, happy, nurturing, and instructive. Good teachers know that discipline goes far beyond what to do when children misbehave: how you handle the situation can help kids choose to behave next time.

The 4 Disciplinary Styles

Discipline is carried out in many different ways. Parents should feel comfortable with developing their own style. But remember, your way may reflect how you were parented as a child. So you may need to rethink it and make some adjustments. Parenting, or disciplinary, style is determined by how responsive and how demanding you are toward children. The 4 disciplinary styles are

1. **Authoritative** parents are equally responsive and demanding. Home life is like a democracy. The kids vote in certain decisions and feel welcome to express their feelings and opinions, yet they understand the limits set by their parents. Parents tend to explain the reasons for rules, discussing expectations and consequences for misbehavior. They also tend to use more positive forms of discipline, have a good relationship with their child, and be very supportive and nurturing.

   Examples of what an authoritative parent would say include
   — "I'm cooking dinner. We have broccoli, salad, or green beans. Which one would you like?"
   — "You have to practice piano, read, and exercise today. What do you want to do first?"
   — "You seem upset. Are you OK?"
   — "Those are good ideas, but I think this is best for now. We'll talk more about it later and come up with a plan together."

2. **Authoritarian** parents are characterized by strict rules, punishment, and little warmth. Home life is like a dictatorship—control and fear rule the day. Parents fall short in the responsive department but reign supreme in demanding what they want from their children. Children are to be controlled, with little to no choices, explanations, or negotiation. The focus of discipline is to punish "bad" behavior. Does this family remind you of the Allens?

   Examples of what an authoritarian parent would say include
   — "You eat what I cook."
   — "Go practice piano, then ride your bike. We'll read later."
   — "Stop crying."
   — "No, do it like this."

3. **Permissive** parents are "pushovers" when it comes to their children. Home life is lawless and lenient. Parents are super responsive, with low demands, because anything goes. They love and nurture their kids very well but have little expectations believing children will figure things out on their own. The kids generally have no rules and can come and go as they please and do as they wish.

    Examples of what a permissive parent would say include
    — "Just French fries? OK."
    — "What are you doing today?"
    — "Come to Mommy, my poor baby. I'm sorry I hurt your feelings."
    — "Do what you think is best. I know you'll figure it out."

4. A **neglectful** parent is an uninvolved parent. This parent gets a zero on both the responsive and demanding scales. Home life can be lonely for the child because the parent doesn't meet emotional needs very well. There is little parent-child relationship, communication, or discipline, but the parent does take care of physical needs such as food, water, and shelter.

    These are examples of a neglectful parent.
    — The child eats whatever is available in the home because meals aren't regularly cooked.
    — The child spends most of their time in their room, doing whatever they want, and doesn't interact much with their parent.
    — The parent seems uninterested or ignores the child when they try to share, try to talk, or are visibly upset.
    — The parent is unaware of any dilemmas the child might be facing and therefore misses opportunities to offer guidance and support.

Which parenting style seems to fit you best? I'm authoritarian by nature and nurture—I was raised that way, remember—but with years of learning and practice, I have moved the needle to a more authoritative parenting style. I'm intentional about being more responsive and allowing my son to have choices, voice his opinion, and have answers to the annoying "Why?" (I still fight the urge to say, "Because I said so.") The authoritative style promotes positive behavior, supports healthy relationships, and is more conducive to a happy and "whole" child who will flourish in life. I saw that change in my son and also see it in families who I encourage to use positive parenting in their home life.

Children raised in an authoritarian home have been shown to be less happy and less friendly, struggle in relationships and peer interactions, have lower self-confidence and poorer conflict resolution, and are prone to depression, anger, and substance problems. All of that control and lack of connection creates more dysfunction and impairment than we could ever know.

Children of permissive parents may lack self-control and self-discipline because of an upbringing without rules, expectations, limits, and structure. Neglectful parenting is regarded as the most damaging, because children are deprived of the attention, nurturing, and love valued by all humans. These children have difficulty forming healthy relationships.

To sum it all up: authoritative parents are more likely to raise happy, healthy, well-behaved children. You may have heard of the "helicopter" or "tiger" mom or "free-range" parent as newer versions of the traditional disciplinarians. In the parenting book *Raising Kids to Thrive*, author Kenneth R. Ginsburg, MD, MS Ed, FAAP, coins the authoritative style–balanced parenting that fosters just the right mix of dependence and independence in children. "Lighthouse parents," as he calls them, are easily seen from the shoreline as a beacon of light to guide children to safety. They make sure their child doesn't crash against the rocks yet permit them to ride the waves even when the water gets rough. They are present to guide and ensure safety. He says that lighthouse parents balance unconditional love with realistic expectations. Be a lighthouse for your child.

What Happens When Different Parenting Styles Exist?

What happens when you have different parenting styles within a home? Well, several things can go wrong. First, the adults may have tension over how best to handle problems with the kids, leading to relational drama. For example, Mom is more authoritative and wants to teach Dennis the right words to use instead of using "potty words." On the other hand, Dad is a die-hard authoritarian and thinks a good, hard spanking will cure the problem. And to make matters worse, if a grandparent is in the home, they may be overly permissive and laugh at the potty words and say, "It's OK, he'll outgrow it."

Secondly, children are likely aware of these conflicts and hear the mixed messages, which undermine your parental authority. It's a form of inconsistency. For example, Dennis is getting 3 different messages. From Mom: I can say, "I passed gas, excuse me," but not "fart." From Grandma: I can say whatever I want because grandma thinks it's funny. From Dad: I'm scared to say the wrong things around Dad.

Lastly, children learn to divide and conquer when parents aren't on the same page. For instance, Dennis always goes to Grandma to ask for things because she always lets him do what he wants. He tries his best to steer clear of Dad or hide misbehavior because he fears the consequences. To stay out of trouble, he often tells his dad or mom, "Grandma said I could," even when she didn't, because he knows she will protect him. All of this confusion is setting Dennis up for lying, manipulation, and a lack of discipline.

What parents and grandparents should do is work through their parenting style differences in private. Never undermine each other in front of the child. Always maintain a united front. In the moment, if you absolutely disagree with what the other is doing, take a pause, step away together, and talk through the issue away from your child.

Children do their best when they have clear and consistent structure, routines, rules, and expectations set by their caregiver. As parents, you have to decide on your parenting style together. You may have different views, but you need to compromise and come together for the benefit of your child. Try your best to balance your styles toward an authoritative approach since that is the style shown to be most effective in building happy, healthy, well-behaved kids and adults who are successful in relationships and life.

Types of Discipline

The following reminder exemplifies what positive and negative discipline look like:

Positive Parenting: Healthy and Effective

- Model appropriate behavior.
- Set limits and rules.
- Establish structure and routines.
- Be proactive.
- Have realistic expectations.
- Redirect.
- Praise efforts and proper behavior.
- Teach wise decision-making.
- Talk the behavior and solutions out.
- Listen.
- Give choices.
- Give rewards.
- Spend "time in" and call time-out.
- Give consequences.
- Remove privileges.

Negative Discipline: Unhealthy and Ineffective

- Spanking
- Hitting
- Shaming
- Controlling
- Name-calling
- Threatening
- Isolating
- Yelling
- Neglecting (emotionally or physically)

 MYTH

Discipline equals spanking.

FACT

Discipline is much more than spanking. Spanking is a type of physical discipline that is not recommended because it is ineffective and harms children.

Physical Discipline

So we're all on the same page, spanking, also known as corporal punishment or physical punishment, is defined by the American Academy of Pediatrics policy statement on discipline as "noninjurious, open-handed hitting with the intention of modifying child behavior." The American Academy of Pediatrics advises against physical punishment and verbal abuse of children. It recommends that disciplinary strategies throughout childhood and adolescence be both positive and effective.

Physical punishment can also be defined as using force intended to cause a child bodily pain or discomfort in order to correct or punish misbehavior. This includes open-handed hitting and heavier physical force, such as hitting with objects. It also includes practices causing children physical discomfort, such as washing their mouth with soap, biting or hitting a child back, forcing a child to hold painful positions, and prolonged exercise. Physical punishment has many names—for example, *tap, hit, pop, smack, slap, punch, spank, beat, paddle, whip, whup,* and *discipline.*

The American Psychological Association "Resolution on Physical Discipline of Children by Parents" opposes corporal punishment as well. It states that physical discipline is associated with

- Increased risk for harm to children's mental health
- Increased risk for harm to cognitive, behavioral, social, and emotional development
- Adverse outcomes across all racial, ethnic, and socioeconomic groups

In addition, the American Academy of Child and Adolescent Psychiatry Child Maltreatment and Violence Committee discourages using corporal punishment to modify behavior. It encourages parents to find other ways to manage child behavior positively.

In 1989, the United Nations Committee on the Rights of the Child called on all member states to ban corporal punishment of children and institute educational programs on positive parenting.

According to both UNICEF and the Global Initiative to End All Corporal Punishment of Children, about 60 countries, states, and territories worldwide have adopted legislation prohibiting corporal punishment against children. However, in the United States, corporal punishment is legal in all states. Most states have banned it in public schools, but 19 still allow it as an option.

In the 1970s, spanking was a widely accepted form of discipline, with parenting experts even advising parents on how to spank appropriately. Moving forward to the '90s, we learn that 80% of parents reported spanking their children. Currently, parents are shifting away from believing it's OK to hit their children and feel bad when they do. Recent polls show that around 67% of parents have spanked and 33% haven't, with mostly younger parents comprising the smaller group. Nowadays, it would be rare to find a pediatrician or parenting expert who approves of spanking or suggests it improves child behavior. And even churches are weighing in. The General Assembly of the Presbyterian Church and United Methodist Church advise their members not to discipline with corporal punishment.

Still, most parents use spanking as a form of discipline. In the United States, 76% of men and 65% of women agreed that "it's sometimes necessary to discipline a child with a good hard spanking," as reported by Child Trends in 2014. No one race or ethnicity spanks as a whole. Some individuals spank and some don't, within all cultures. That said, statistically, Black parents spank at a higher percentage, followed by Hispanic parents, then White parents, and finally Asian parents, according to child discipline expert Elizabeth T. Gershoff, PhD. Other factors she reported that increase the likelihood of a parent spanking include

- Lower income
- Educational level
- Cultural and religious beliefs that normalize spanking
- Frequent parental frustration with the child
- A parent younger than 30 years
- Parents who have a toddler or preschool-aged child
- A parent who is personally stressed
- Parents who were spanked themselves

As a Black mother and pediatrician who cares for a diverse patient population, I've noticed how Black parents lean heavily on spanking their kids and are more resistant to stopping or reducing it to some degree. I've heard over and over again, "If I don't spank him, they will." There's this overwhelming, internalized fear that makes Black parents desperate to force their children to behave in order to protect them from an unjust world. A world that, historically, has been traumatic for people of color, from slavery to modern forms of racism and discrimination, such as harsher school discipline, police brutality, and mass incarceration. One where a single mistake can be unforgiving and even deadly. Black parents sometimes overcompensate because they believe their kids can't afford to misbehave, which doesn't seem to be the case for their white counterparts. Black parents overreact because they are fighting to defy stereotypes and they want their kids to represent their race and culture in the best possible light at all times.

I call this "harsh, save-my-kid" discipline—a survival mindset. Although it comes from a place of love and protection, it's just as dangerous and harmful as the very thing parents are trying to protect their child from. It also perpetuates the legacy of trauma from our past. So to my fellow Black parents, the world will pose injustices and dangers to our kids. What they need to build resilience and overcome this "mean old world" is a thriving mindset—our love, support, and guidance—not more of the same.

In *Spare the Kids: Why Whupping Children Won't Save Black America,* author, journalist, and professor Stacey Patton challenges the cultural tradition of corporal punishment in Black homes. One of the most poignant points from her book is that spanking was not an African tradition; rather, it was taught to enslaved Africans through false narratives in Christianity and slavery. This book is necessary reading for Black parents to understand and help stop the cycle of violence in our homes.

MYTH

If you don't spank your kids, they'll be bad, spoiled, and unsuccessful in life—"Spare the rod, spoil the child."

 FACT

The evidence is clear. Spanking is ineffective and harmful. It can lead to behavioral, emotional, and mental health problems in children. The rod is a symbol of discipline, guidance, and protection, not a literal rod meant to hit misbehaving kids.

Overwhelming evidence cited by the American Academy of Pediatrics has shown that negative forms of discipline hurt children. Individuals who experienced physical punishment as a child are more likely to

- Spank their own children
- Hit a spouse or conflict maritally as adults
- Engage in higher rates of substance use and be at increased risk for crime and violence when exposed as older children and adolescents
- Have reduced prefrontal cortical gray matter and lower performance IQ
- Have elevated levels of the stress hormone cortisol, which have been shown to change brain structure

 MYTH

Yelling, threatening, or shaming is less harmful.

 FACT

Verbal abuse or harsh words can be just as harmful and hurtful as physical discipline, and the effects, more long-lasting.

❌ **MYTH**

Parents should control their children with old-school discipline phrases like "Do as I say, not as I do"; "Do what I say, when I say, and how I say"; "Because I said so"; and "Kids should be seen and not heard." Children behave when they fear their parents.

✅ **FACT**

Parental control stunts child development, learning, and independence. Kids shouldn't fear their parents. They should choose to behave because they love, trust, and respect their parents.

Nonphysical Discipline

Harsh verbal correction, as well as emotional and physical neglect, is just as harmful to kids as physical punishment. This includes parental behaviors that shame, put down, humiliate, threaten, scare, or are overly aggressive toward the child. A longitudinal study showed that harsh verbal abuse before the age of 13 years was associated with increased adolescent conduct problems and symptoms of depression between the ages of 13 and 14. Another study showed white matter differences in the brains of young adults who were exposed to parental verbal abuse.

Use of Control

Parenting by force, threat, or fear is a control tactic or coercive behavior, which is also a negative form of discipline. Positive parenting should be more about guiding and steering your kids in the right direction. Consider what I heard in a parenting class: the behavior analyst Tara Concelman says, "You don't control your child. The child decides if they will or won't do it." I experienced this with my daughter when she was 2. She definitely had the upper hand when it came to what she chose to eat and when she chose to sleep. And don't even get me started on the potty training! I know some of you authoritarian parents are clutching your pearls and screaming, "Not in my house!" But take a deep breath and hear me out. The control you think you have is disappearing every day as your child strives for independence and grows into a freethinking teen and young adult.

Controlling your child holds them back. It stifles their ability to be creative, confident, self-determined, independent, and responsible. Do you want robot-like kids or competent, self-directed kids? Do you hope for an employee or a blooming founder or CEO? And do you want them either whole and happy or crippled and miserably codependent? Parents want their children to gain the ability to self-manage and choose to behave appropriately. We want them ready to go out into the world—confident and ready to think for themselves!

Tara also says, "You can only control yourself and the environment." That's it! You can manage your emotions, expectations, and actions in dealing with your child's behavior and adjust the environment around you to influence better behavior. You can encourage their choice to do what you ask. With support, guidance, and proactive adjustments, your child will be set up to make positive choices. Parent tricks at their finest. More on these later.

All of these negative forms of discipline just aren't worthwhile. Especially because there are alternative strategies that work without the lifelong baggage. Remember, what happens in childhood, doesn't stay in childhood.

Contrary to popular belief, negative discipline doesn't work to correct behavior! It may stop misbehavior in the moment. But long-term behaviors usually repeat because

1. The child learns little about what they did wrong or how to make better choices in the future.
2. The child is likely to feel angry, hurt, resentful, and discouraged to do better, which turns the focus away from what was done wrong initially and hurts your relationship with the child.
3. The child gets used to frequent spankings and threats over time. Parents then escalate their actions, creating an environment that can lead to child abuse.

The truth is, some parents use physical discipline and other controlling strategies because this is what they were taught. Some parents just don't know what else to do when they become frustrated and angry with their child. So think about the positive and negative aspects of your childhood. Hopefully, those will help you rethink how you choose to discipline your own children—fingers crossed.

In the parts to come, you'll find more positive alternatives to use in managing the day-to-day stressors of parenting your children when they misbehave. And once you complete this book, you will be well equipped to apply the best discipline strategies that work for your child.

❌ **MYTH**

When children misbehave, they should be punished.

✅ **FACT**

When children misbehave, they should be taught the correct behavior. Consequences can be used to discourage and correct misbehavior, but punishing your child should not be the goal.

❌ **MYTH**

Disobedience and nonadherence equal disrespect and are intentional.

✅ **FACT**

Misbehavior is not about you. So don't take it personally. The child is thinking only of what they want (and struggling to do the right thing or what you want).

Why Is Discipline Needed?

I think we all know that children need discipline. Children come into this world with a blank slate. They can't tell right from wrong or don't have the experience of adults. They don't know that pulling the dog's tail or eating a Tide laundry detergent pod is unsafe. Children don't know that picking their nose is gross, nor do they care. Parents are responsible for teaching their children appropriate behaviors, keeping them safe, correcting misbehaviors, and helping them gain self-control. And we make it all happen through discipline.

Children raised with appropriate discipline are more likely to take responsibility for their actions, have self-confidence, help others, establish friendships, and have positive decision-making. On the other hand, children raised without discipline have difficulty with behaving appropriately, respecting authority, making friends, and developing life skills. Discipline is as necessary as food, water, and shelter.

It's also important to know why children misbehave before we discuss how to discipline them. Early in childhood, children have difficulty keeping their hands to themselves or taking turns playing with toys. These are "I don't know better" misbehaviors. Children also misbehave when parental expectations and instructions are unclear. Today this behavior is OK, tomorrow it's not. Consistency and clear expectations are very important, and they're the parents' responsibility.

Sometimes children do unwanted things because they want something or want to do something that is in conflict with adult wishes. For instance, young children are biologically evolved to defy the rules of authority as part of their typical development. When the child's mind becomes aware that situations can be different, the child will test those options. This drives the defiance of the toddler. What child does not want to eat candy or play video games all day long even though their parent says no. In this case, the child chooses to do what they want despite the consequences. This is defiance or nonadherence.

In other cases, children may act before thinking. This is impulsivity. And younger children may not even have this reasoning capacity yet. Then there is misbehavior that continues because parents fuel it by rewarding the unwanted behavior unintentionally. For example, John is working from home and sees that his toddler Dawn is getting upset because she wants her cookies. However, John realizes it's going to be lunchtime soon, and if he gives her the cookies, she will never eat her lunch. As her cries escalate, John gives in, giving Dawn a cookie to keep the peace and to be able to get his work done. What just happened? John's "No" has become ineffective, and Dawn has learned to use crying and tantrums to get what she wants. Jackpot!

Older kids and teens may misbehave as an act of rebellion. This can be in your face or passive-aggressive in nature. For example, David, a teenager, is very frustrated with his mom's constant criticizing of what he wears. Sandy just wants him to look nice and neat and has gone as far as to make him change clothes and even monitor how he gets his hair cut. After yet another argument, David alters the outfits Sandy bought and dyes his hair purple. What's going on here?

Sandy has created a power struggle that she can't win, nor should she. David should get to choose his personal style with her support and guidance. The root of his misbehavior grew out of fighting for independence and resenting her control. These are warning signs that the parent-child relationship is struggling.

Instead of focusing on the negative behavior, focus on the why. Trying to understand why your child has misbehaved is key to correcting the behavior, preventing it in the future, and guiding how to discipline them.

How to Discipline

When parents provide safe and stable environments with nurturing parent-child relationships, they set the foundation for their children to learn appropriate behavior over time. Consider Dawn again. She will learn to control her emotions as John supports her development, models co-regulation, practices consistency with limit setting, ignores her outbursts, and, when she is calmer, helps her use her words to express her feelings.

All parents want their children to become caring, productive members of society and successful adults. These are some of the short- and long-term goals of discipline. However, we can't forget that how we discipline also has "now" and "later" effects. Disciplinary actions should be effective both in encouraging appropriate behaviors and in extinguishing unwanted behaviors in a way that is helpful, not harmful.

It's like being offered a new medication for a medical problem. If you feel that the side effects or potential harm from the medication (risks) outweigh the chance of a cure (benefits), you won't take the medication. You will ask for alternatives that work and are less harmful. Well, negative forms of discipline are like toxic drugs, with lots of risks and zero, zilch, nada benefits for your child. So please don't use them.

Your job as a parent or other caregiver is to teach your child how to behave, keep them safe, and promote healthy development. That's not an easy task. And kids don't come with instructions on how to do it. It certainly takes time, patience, and understanding. But any job gets easier with proper training. By learning peaceful, positive strategies, you will help your child learn to behave as they grow.

The following diagram displays the 5 essential puzzle pieces to help establish a positive and effective family discipline plan, what I call the High Five Essentials, and poses some questions:

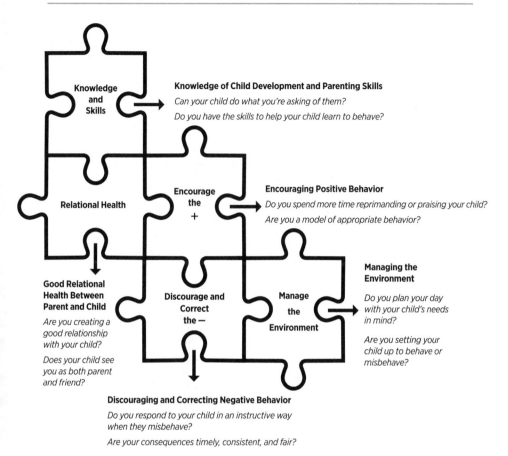

Knowledge of Child Development and Parenting Skills

Can your child do what you're asking of them?

Do you have the skills to help your child learn to behave?

Encouraging Positive Behavior

Do you spend more time reprimanding or praising your child?

Are you a model of appropriate behavior?

Managing the Environment

Do you plan your day with your child's needs in mind?

Are you setting your child up to behave or misbehave?

Good Relational Health Between Parent and Child

Are you creating a good relationship with your child?

Does your child see you as both parent and friend?

Discouraging and Correcting Negative Behavior

Do you respond to your child in an instructive way when they misbehave?

Are your consequences timely, consistent, and fair?

Don't worry, we'll dive into the specifics of these important elements of discipline in the coming chapters. Putting the pieces together . . .

Parenting Prescription

Maximize positive parenting and minimize negative discipline!

Chapter 2

A Win-Win Approach: The High Five Essentials of Effective and Positive Parenting

As a group of us sat around Debra and Mike's table, we shared stories about how our parents disciplined us when we were kids. Kenny's parents made him do weird things, like stand on one leg for a long time. After talking and sharing, we figured out that most of us "got whupped" when we were kids. Karen was the only one who was never spanked. I was jealous of her at that moment.

Then the conversation naturally turned to how we discipline our own children. Kenny's wife, Felicia, shared how her son, Brian, got into big trouble recently. Felicia needed to get to work on time, so they were rushing out the door to drop Brian off at summer camp first. Felicia explained that she had to yell at Brian several times to get him to focus on getting ready instead of playing a video game. When they finally arrived at camp, she noticed Brian had on only one shoe. Admittedly, she lost it! She yelled and "swatted" him a few times. A camp counselor witnessed the hitting but turned and quickly tiptoed away. Later, Felicia talked with Kenny and they decided to put Brian on punishment (I don't remember how long exactly, but it was a long time). I think the general consensus from our group was that this was appropriate discipline and Brian deserved it, because he chose to play video games instead of following his mom's instructions to get dressed, which made her late for work. I suppressed the urge to explain that his punishment was too harsh and the whole situation could have been avoided.

Then Mike, who always asks deep, philosophical questions, just had to ask me, the pediatrician, "Hey Candice, what's the best way to discipline kids?"

At one time or another, parents are puzzled with the best way to discipline their kids. I encourage parents to keep discipline peaceful and positive and learn strategies that work, not hurt. And what works for one child may need to be altered for another. You may remember the essential puzzle pieces mentioned at the end of the previous chapter, what I call the High Five Essentials. Once again, they are

1. Knowledge of Child Development and Parenting Skills
2. Good Relational Health Between Parent and Child
3. Encouraging Positive Behavior
4. Discouraging and Correcting Negative Behavior
5. Managing the Environment

Let's explore these 5 essential pieces as a foundation for solving the discipline puzzle and creating your family discipline plan.

1. Knowledge of Child Development and Parenting Skills

Parental knowledge and parenting skills are so important for the overall health and well-being of children. Why? They equip caregivers to understand what children go through and to empathize with their experiences. They also help set realistic expectations for children and provide appropriate child care and discipline. Where can you gain these? Parenting class!

Parenting classes help you gain valuable knowledge and necessary skills to parent well. Every parent can use a little help in this area. A good parenting class teaches basic child care, which is valuable for first-time parents or those who need an update because times have changed (we don't give infants nursery water or lay infants to sleep on their tummies anymore), as well as reminders for seasoned parents who think they know it all. It also helps parents learn about themselves and reflect on what type of parent and disciplinarian they would like to be. Look for parenting classes in your area by asking your pediatrician, by asking your school counselor, or by calling your local health department, department of child and family, or 211 (the United Way Helpline).

In addition, parents learn about child development, which is an esssential piece of positive parenting. Understanding how children grow and develop helps parents form realistic expectations and meet children where they are, not where we want them to be. And of course, a great parenting class teaches how to discipline properly and gives tons of skills and strategies to manage whatever your child throws your way. You don't need to get a degree, but you should take a parenting class so your discipline foundation is sound.

Understanding child development and developing parenting skills have been shown to improve the lives of families tremendously. If you are expecting a bundle of joy or are already a parent, I encourage you to chat with your pediatrician about parenting and discipline. Pediatricians love to talk about this stuff, and they can provide credible resources or local referrals to help improve your parenting skills.

The following chart shows how various parenting programs have benefited both children and parents:

Parenting program	Description
Connected Kids	American Academy of Pediatrics program to help children grow up safe, strong, and secure. Handouts for caregivers on various parenting topics, such as discipline and development. https://patiented.solutions.aap.org/DocumentLibrary/ Connected%20Kids%20Clinical%20Guide.pdf
Bright Futures	Follows American Academy of Pediatrics guidelines for health supervision of infants, children, and teens. Child development, parenting, and discipline information for parents provided by the pediatrician. https://brightfutures.aap.org/families
Help Me Grow	Promotes early identification of developmental, behavioral, or educational concerns and then connects children and families to community-based services and support at no cost to parents and other caregivers https://helpmegrownational.org
Healthy Start	Focuses on the health and well-being of a mother and baby. Provides parenting classes, newborn care, car seat instruction, nurse visits, and more. https://mchb.hrsa.gov/maternal-child-health-initiatives/ healthy-start
Local health department	Provides "Bellies, Babies and Beyond" program, Healthy Families program, visiting nurse partnership, and more to improve the health of families and communities
211	United Way program that provides information on local services. Call this help line for immediate resources and assistance, and a specialist in your area will follow up with you.

(continued on next page)

Parenting program	Description
The Triple P – Positive Parenting Program	Parenting program developed by clinical psychologist and professor Matt Sanders to prevent and manage behavior and emotional problems in children and teenagers. Parents reported less stress, depression, and use of coercive parenting. Children experienced reduced abuse rates, foster care placement, and behavior and emotional problems. www.triplep-parenting.com
The Incredible Years Parenting Pyramid	Parenting program developed by clinical psychologist Carolyn Webster-Stratton, MS, MPH, PhD, to prevent and treat young children's behavior issues and promote social, emotional, and academic knowledge. Successful with culturally diverse groups. Increases nurturing parenting, decreases harsh discipline, improves parental involvement in school, and decreases behavior problems. www.incredibleyears.com
Center for the Improvement of Child Caring	Founded by clinical psychologist Kerby Alvy, PhD, to focus on a positive approach to parenting, upholding the rights of children and helping caregivers gain effective disciplinary skills. Provides the following national model programs in parenting skill building: • New Confident Parenting Program for parents of all cultural backgrounds • Effective Black Parenting Program for parents of Black children • Los Ninos Bien Educados Program for parents of Latino children Increases parental confidence, stress reduction and management, and parenting skills. Reduces or eliminates the use of spanking and hitting. Improves parent-child relationships, reduces child behavior problems, and increases child adherence. www.ciccparenting.org

Parenting program	Description
Conscious Discipline	An evidence-based, trauma-informed parent education curriculum by Becky Bailey, PhD, shown to improve parenting knowledge and skills, increase parental self-control, and improve child behavior and emotional regulation. "Parents reported feeling happier, less frustrated and more interested in connecting with their children." https://consciousdiscipline.com/parent-education-curriculum-designated-research-based
Centers for Disease Control and Prevention Parent Information	Aged-based parenting advice, resources, and videos www.cdc.gov/parents

You may have noticed that this section doesn't cover specifics on child development and parenting skills. Don't worry, this is just an introduction. Part 4, Act Like a Parent but Think Like a Child, gets into all the juicy details to help you discipline well.

2. Good Relational Health Between Parent and Child

Building a positive, nurturing parent-child relationship is a key factor in achieving a well-behaved child. It's also important for the overall health and well-being of the child. Good relational health supports child development in areas of communication, emotional control, and social skills. In addition, positive relationships are the

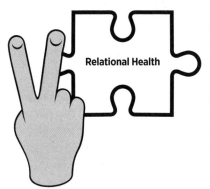

foundation of building trust, which children need to follow our lead as adults and even come to us for help. A healthy relationship supports independence in the maturing child but maintains connection for when coaching, guiding, and protection are needed. As well, it demonstrates how to handle conflict in a kind, respectful, and understanding way. Perhaps the family's greatest strength is relationship.

Children experience their first and most significant relationship with a parent, which serves as the basis for all other relationships that follow. The parent-child relationship develops in early infancy through bonding and secure attachment. Parents love their children dearly from the time they are in the womb and, at first sight, respond by holding, kissing, feeding, changing, and singing to them. An infant begins to learn to feel safe and secure with loving parents who meet their needs, thus building trust and love. Over time, this loving and supportive relationship is tested as children strive for independence and test limits set by their parents. Toddlers throw tantrums when Mommy says no to the toy in the store. Children refuse and talk back when Daddy tells them to stop the video game after playing for 2 straight hours. And teens yell and scream when their phone privileges are revoked for inappropriate texting. If these conversations are managed improperly, the child's resistant behaviors and refusal to obey, coupled with parental disappointment and frustration, can create a stressful, hostile, and dysfunctional home environment. And this environment is what chips away at the relationship. It happens to us all. No family is free from conflict. No parent is perfect. Sometimes parents get discipline right and sometimes they get it wrong. But hang in there, and don't ever give up. Even though our children may think they are mature enough, they still need us for guidance and support.

Consider the following questions as a way to gauge the strength of your current relationship with your child:

Yes	No	
☐	☐	Can your child come to you about anything?
☐	☐	Do you accept your child as they are?
☐	☐	Do you respect your child's opinions?
☐	☐	Do you allow your child to choose?
☐	☐	Do you encourage your child to express their feelings?
☐	☐	Do you enjoy spending time with your child?
☐	☐	Do you get along well with your child?
☐	☐	Do you resolve conflict with your child fully and peacefully?

How did you do? If your child is old enough to understand, ask these same questions, from their perspective, to check whether you both are on the same page. If your child is not old enough yet, be sure to be intentional about strengthening your relationship in these areas. Actually, these questions are good to take inventory of any relationship! I did pretty well with my son, but there is room for improvement. For instance, my son and I have a love-hate relationship when it comes to electronics and gaming. He loves them and I hate them. It causes major conflict within our home. As a pediatrician, I know all the downsides of excessive gaming and screen time, so I set rules and limitations to protect him. As a child, he lacks understanding of these rules and tests those limits often.

Media Use Guidelines for Children by the American Academy of Pediatrics

▶ Children younger than 18 months: Using screen media other than video chatting should be discouraged.

▶ Children 18 to 24 months of age: Parents who want to introduce digital media should choose high-quality programming and apps and use them together with children, because this interaction is how toddlers learn best.

▶ Children 2 to 5 years of age: Limit screen time to an hour a day. Parents should co-watch and discuss content with their child.

▶ Children 6 years and older: Parents should set limits on screen time and types of media. Don't allow screen time to interrupt sleep, exercise, or other healthy habits.

Parents should designate media-free times together, like dinner, and media-free zones, like kids' bedrooms. Children should not be allowed to have TVs, computers, smartphones, or similar devices in their bedrooms. Parents can't always monitor these devices 24/7.

Create a family media use plan at www.healthychildren.org/English/media.

What I struggle with the most is he constantly wants to talk to me about the games and he requests that I play them with him. I realize that this is an amazing opportunity for us to connect and strengthen our relationship. However, it's not easy, because I'm terribly disinterested and despise these games. I discussed with him my plan to allow time for us to play together or at least talk about the games briefly on the weekends. You would have thought he won the lottery! He was so excited and even said later, "Thanks, Mom, for playing the games with me, because I know you don't really like it." And ironically, it made enforcing the screen time rules much easier and more successful, because he seems to appreciate my effort. And when he points out I've been shopping for a little too long, I quickly remind him of my gaming sacrifice, and that ends the protest. It's a win-win. And I love that he's learning to compromise. For younger children, it's as simple as comforting their boo-boos, staying with them until they fall asleep because they're afraid of the dark, understanding their excessive energy and fiery temperament, being patient enough to let them try a difficult task all on their own just because they want to, and tolerating the mess for the sake of their learning a new skill.

So how do we build and maintain a healthy relationship with our children that can stand the test of time? By focusing on the following 7 areas:

Love and Affection

I talk with parents about the strong love they have for their children. I challenge them to let their actions speak louder than their words when it comes to love in the home. It's wonderful to say "I love you." But it's equally important to show love, act with love, speak with love, and discipline with love. For me, love is a verb!

I also recommend the book *The 5 Love Languages of Children* by Gary Chapman and Ross Campbell to parents, because it helped me tremendously to strengthen my relationship with my son, as I am sure it has helped others. The love languages of Physical Touch, Words of Affirmation, Quality Time, Receiving Gifts, and Acts of Service are the same for children and adults. Once you fill your child's love tank by speaking their love language, your relationship will flourish and go the distance, just as a car whose tank you've filled.

What I gained from this book is that your love for your child should be unconditional and not based on what they do or don't do or whether they're right or wrong. You should show them the same amount of love when they're wonderful as when they're wrong. No matter how bad things get or how stressful things become, you can still handle your child's behavior in a loving way. Parents and other caregivers are the models for kids on how they should love and be loved. If children don't receive or witness the love they deserve at home, they won't have a model of how they should be treated or behave in relationships with others.

To fully connect with your children, you must understand what makes them feel loved and provide it as often as possible. Talk with your children about this. I learned that my son feels loved when I watch a silly movie with him or when he wrestles with his dad. He smiles with joy when he snuggles close to me. And then I notice that for the rest of the day, he is more likely to follow my instructions.

He also feels loved when he receives the simplest gifts, like a smoothie after school or time on the Xbox. But the most effective tool I have in my parenting toolbox is words to encourage and praise him. He responds beautifully to positive words. They change his attitude and behavior when things are going wrong. They also encourage him to continue when "it's all good."

So it looks like my son's love languages are Words of Affirmation, Quality Time, and Receiving Gifts. I truly believe that loving your child according to how they feel loved and perceive love (ie, their love language) will strengthen their love for you. Your connection and relationship will flourish. Your child will feel safe and secure with you, trust you, listen to you, and behave for you to make you happy and proud of them. You won't have to force positive behavior.

Take the following quiz with your child to learn how to fill their tank with love: www.5lovelanguages.com/profile/children.

Honesty

Honesty between a parent and child about feelings, concerns, and shortcomings is crucial. Be vulnerable and let your children get to know you and your life experiences. I know you may worry that what you share will be thrown in your face later, but take the chance, because even that can be a lesson learned. For instance, when Abby becomes upset after losing a soccer game, her mom understands and shares how she herself got over losing softball games as a child.

Being honest makes you human, more relatable and approachable, in your child's eyes. They will feel that they can come to you for anything without being judged. This builds trust and promotes mutual honesty and acceptance.

Respect

All children deserve respect as humans. It's important for us parents to show respect to children by treating them like we would want to be treated. Consider your child's feelings before you act or speak even when you're angry at something they may have done. You should express your disappointment respectfully and encourage them to share their feelings as well.

Let your child know what you admire about them. Share your appreciation of how kind they are to everyone and how helpful they are around the house. Be specific and list some things they have recently done. Express how proud you are of them and how lucky you are to have them in your life. This lets them know "I see you!" If you respect your child, they will respect you.

Connection

Having a good connection is all about getting closer to your child and finding ways to relate to each other. Focus on spending quality time together, even if it's brief. Get creative. Simple things, like reading a bedtime story together, and big events, like going to a concert together, all matter to strengthen the parent-child connection.

Perhaps the most common concerns of children that weaken connection are that parents don't listen and parents just don't understand (one of my "fave" tunes from the '90s). And when children don't feel heard and understood, they feel frustrated, they shut down, and they are less likely to understand your point of view. So parents, don't talk so much, and take the time to listen to what your children are saying! Don't take over every conversation. Allow your child to fully express themselves. Encourage your children to share their feelings by asking, "How does that make you feel?" Ask open-ended questions like "What do you think about . . . ?" so they can't answer with just a simple yes or no.

In addition, it is very important to give your child time to respond to open-ended questions. Research shows that parents usually give kids 1 to 2 seconds to answer an open-ended question. Kids often need 5 to 10 seconds to understand, process, and formulate an answer to an open-ended question, which has an infinite number of responses. This is called "wait time," a term coined by researcher Mary Budd Rowe. Asking open-ended questions and allowing wait time will help you truly get to know your child, what's important to them, and their likes and dislikes. This approach builds autonomy, confidence, and esteem in your child because they will feel that their opinions matter to you. It also models empathy—understanding by walking a mile in someone else's shoes.

Reciprocity, or responding to a positive action in a similar way, is also important to invest in your relationship with your child. It starts as early as infancy when a baby coos and smiles and Mom or Dad or another caregiver chuckles and responds. As your child grows, reciprocity continues. It's important in connection and the development of communication and social skills. So smile when your child smiles, hug back when they reach for a hug, and sit quietly with them, even when they don't feel like talking.

Having a little fun is always a good way to connect. Play with your kids. Playing is so much more than fun. It's quality time and also a sneaky way for kids to learn. It literally enhances brain development, social skills, and cognitive skills in children. From playing with rattles and keys on a tummy time mat to a game of Twister when you're stuck inside on a rainy day, don't forget to make playtime a priority.

Belonging

A sense of belonging is something children want, just like adults. Besides being seen and heard, they need to feel as if they are wanted and needed. They need to feel accepted. Even though you may disagree with your child sometimes, acceptance is all about understanding, which strengthens belonging and relationship. Make sure your child feels like an important member of your family unit by showing and telling them. Give your child the responsibility of helping maintain the home environment by doing age-appropriate chores around the house. Let them vote on family decisions, such as where to eat dinner or where to go on summer vacation.

Belonging is important emotionally. Without it, children feel lonely or isolated. A sense of belonging says you are not alone and we are in this together.

Support

Children need adult support to live, learn, and grow. Parental support communicates to children that we have their back and they can depend on us. It's also important to the success of the child because it promotes self-confidence, self-worth, and overall mental well-being.

Here are ways to support your child.

- Let them know that you're there for them if they need you or need to talk. Ask whether they're doing OK.
- Encourage and attend their activities.
- Be involved with their education and at the school.
- Assist with problems, such as homework or conflict with friends.
- Give responsibilities, such as house chores or walking the dog.
- Give positive feedback and constructive criticism. For example, say,
  —"I like how you shared some of your treat with your sister."
  —"Next time, remember to thank everyone."

A Friendly Relationship

My first response to my friend Mike's question about the best way to discipline children was to have a good relationship with your child. Whenever I say that, parents say, "Parents shouldn't be friends with their kids." But they're missing the point. Yes, parents should have friendly relationships with their children, which include playtimes and fun times together. It is good for parents and kids to "like" each other and enjoy each other's company, which builds positive emotional bonding. That said, this does not mean parents should give up parental authority, expectations, and boundaries. You are the authority figure: the person your child should be able to trust, talk with about anything, and have adventures with.

I can't stress enough how important it is to have a good relationship with your child. If you want your child to behave, strengthen your relationship with them. They will try very hard to adhere, because they trust you, love you, and don't want to disappoint you! I don't agree with shaming children, but applying a little disappointment is helpful when you have a strong, positive relationship. You could say something like "I'm so disappointed that you chose to lie about your homework. When you tell the truth, people will trust you and so will I. Now let's get your homework done." **Love and affection, honesty, respect, connection, belonging, support,** and **a friendly relationship** with your child are all parts of the Good Relational Health Between Parent and Child piece of the discipline puzzle. Trust me, having a strong, positive parent-child relationship makes discipline much easier for a parent and child.

3. Encouraging Positive Behavior

Tiffany came in frequently to the clinic with little Melody. Melody always had a feisty temperament and was advanced for her age. This particular day, she was moving all over the examination room—opening the cabinets, lifting the trash

can lid, and climbing the step stool. I could hear Tiffany yelling, "No, don't . . . stop it!" about 10 times over 10 minutes before I entered the room. And you guessed it, Melody also started yelling, "No!" and "Stop it!"

"Hey, Tiffany. How are you? Toddler life, huh?" I said. She shook her head without saying a word, as if she were too tired and frustrated to explain. Trying to lighten her load, I explained, "Most toddlers are this busy and sassy. Hang in there. Family life will get better. Let's discuss some strategies that can help."

First, I noticed that Tiffany hadn't realized that Melody was doing more things right than wrong. I pointed out to her that Melody was following my examination instructions beautifully, that she had greeted me in such a kind way, and that her "busyness" was just a typical toddler exploring and playing in a small room while waiting for the doctor. She wasn't being "bad." She was being perfect! But I do realize that some parents just don't understand, and the energy of toddlers can deplete and frustrate us.

Positive Reinforcement

I gave Tiffany several recommendations, one being the use of positive reinforcement. It's a form of discipline that encourages proper behavior by giving a reward right after that behavior occurs to increase the chance that the child will do more of it. When you positively reinforce, you consistently try to "catch your child being good." Spending your time by acknowledging and responding to "good" behavior gives your child the attention and connection they so desperately want and need.

Positive reinforcement is such a valuable discipline strategy, because it builds on what is already good inside the child. These days, everyone loves taking selfies, right? Well, positive reinforcement is the GOAT (greatest of all time) of selfies! Why? Because using it fosters **self**-confidence, **self**-esteem, **self**-worth, **self**-determination, and **self**-empowerment in children. They become more independent and more connected to us when we focus on the good they do.

The reward is not a payoff for proper behavior (bribes are before and rewards are after). It doesn't have to be anything monetary or a sweet treat. Keep it simple and specific to what your child responds favorably to. A smile, a nod, a high five, or some other praise for what they've just done so well. Your attention and the fact that you're focusing on the best they have to offer are all it takes to help them do more of it. We all want children to clean up after themselves, use good manners, tie their own shoes, and eat their vegetables. Try positive reinforcement to entice kids into practicing early skills and continuing good habits they've already mastered. Notice their attempt, praise their effort, and watch their skill grow.

Here are different types of positive reinforcers that can be used to encourage proper behavior.

- **Natural reinforcers** occur directly because of the behavior (ie, study hard for a test and get a good grade, practice basketball and become better at it, and organize your closet and feel proud of yourself). Natural reinforcers foster self-esteem and self-motivation.
- **Social reinforcers** require the attention of others to recognize or approve the behavior. Compliments, encouragement, and rewards are all examples of social reinforcers. They may seem shallow to some but strongly fulfill the need for acceptance and belonging.
- As children get older, **token reinforcers,** or incentives, can be used to leverage rewards for proper behavior. They're like dangling a carrot to lead a horse to water. If the horse follows and reaches the water, it will have the water plus a nice, sweet carrot. If not, oh well. Try again. Daily or weekly behavior charts that accumulate points or tokens are good examples of this strategy. They're great to motivate kids to behave, because the child can see the benefits of their efforts. Sit down with your child and create your own chart (see the example later on this page). You can even customize it with artwork of your child's favorite characters. List the behavior goals for your child and discuss these with them so they understand what each goal is.

My Weekly Reward Chart

Tasks	Mon	Tue	Wed	Thu	Fri	Sat	Sun
"Get ready" routine (morning and night)		☆					
Keep my space tidy	☆		☆				
Be kind to others	☆	☆	☆				
Take a deep breath and use my words		☆	☆				
Follow instructions	☆		☆				

My Daily Goal: ___3 stars___   My Daily Reward: ___Stickers___

My Weekly Goal: ___21 stars___   My Weekly Reward: ___Coins in a money jar___

Use stickers, coins, or anything of value to your child as rewards to note the times when you catch your child being good or meeting goals. You can also use the total number of stickers or coins earned toward a point system or marbles in a jar to give your child a bigger reward at the end of the week or month. Maybe allow the child to choose a movie to watch or a board game to play. Or maybe they can choose a favorite restaurant they want to go to, which gives a sense of autonomy.

That said, this strategy is strictly for motivation and proper behavior. Never, I mean never, take away a reward or threaten to take away a reward that the child earned. Doing so will render this skill useless.

Finally, rewards, such as money or a desired item, can be used to build motivation, but feeling satisfied in a job well done is the goal. As your child gets the hang of doing the things you want them to, such as brushing their teeth, going to bed on time, or completing their homework, you can start to decrease or delay the intervals of rewards. We don't want children to behave well for the reward. We just want to use the reward to get them there and then allow them to keep the behavior going on their own.

Negative Reinforcement

Now, this one can be a little confusing, so read carefully. Negative reinforcement, identified by psychologist B. F. Skinner, is a strategy used to encourage proper behavior by stopping, removing, or avoiding a negative or unfavorable outcome for the child. The child misbehaves. The parent removes a privilege or takes away something the child likes. The child meets expectations to regain the item or privilege. Negative reinforcement is exemplified in the following chart, along with positive reinforcement.

Let's sum it all up! Encourage proper behavior with the following strategies:

Positive reinforcement	Negative reinforcement
Positive feedback or praise—for example, "Great job, I'm so proud of you!" "I like that!" "How do you feel?" "Cool!"	Child has 5 missing assignments at school. He loses video game time until he catches up and turns in all missing assignments.
Behavior chart with stickers or tokens	Child disobeys a nonnegotiable rule and loses parent attention by sitting in a time-out.

Positive reinforcement	Negative reinforcement
Nonverbal praise—for example, smile, nod, fist bump, pat on the back	Teen talks back to parents and argues. Teen loses iPhone for 2 hours while they practice speaking respectfully to their parents.
Rewards—for example, gifts or treats	Child did not wash dishes as told. TV is turned off until all dishes are washed and put away.
Allowance or money earned	Child continues to fight with their siblings. Parents tell the child they can come out of their room when they calm down.

Positive Instructions (Avoiding "No, Stop, Don't . . .")

As for Melody saying "No" to her mom, I explained to Tiffany that it's not an ideal behavior, but it's common among toddlers. Kids don't understand that saying "No" is frowned on, at least not early on. But they do repeat what they see and hear despite the old saying "Do as I say, not as I do." So if Melody's mom wanted her to use the word *no* appropriately, she would have to use it in the right way also.

We discussed the importance of parents reframing their discipline approach by using positive commands when communicating with their children. Like telling them what to do, instead of what not to do. When kids hear "No, stop, don't . . ." all the time, it begins to sound like blah, blah, blah. It loses power and becomes ineffective when we really need it to keep kids safe. Then we feel the need to get louder and harsher, because the child won't listen and follow instructions. But remember, children don't respond if they hear it all the time and will definitely repeat those words to others. So I said, "When the school calls about Melody speaking harshly to her friends, try not to say, 'I have no idea where she got that from. . . .'"

I suggested reserving "No, stop, don't . . ." for when it *really* matters. Like when your child is about to run into the street or tries to stick a fork into an electrical outlet. A forceful "STOP!" can snap them out of making that dangerous choice and save their lives. For everything else, tell or show the child what to do. Showing or telling works and I recommend it to my patients and families often. Check out this chart of positive, common statements to use in place of "No, stop, don't. . . ."

Behavior	Positive response
Playing in the trash	"The trash can is dirty—hands off the trash can, please."
Climbing	"That's not safe. You might fall. Get down."
Hitting or kicking	"Nice hands, please." "Feet on the ground."
Running	"Walking feet. Show me the right way to walk."
Putting things into the mouth	"That's not food, play with it like this."
Drawing on the wall	"Draw on the paper, please."

Remember, when the child follows instructions, always reinforce that behavior with praise. Tiffany and I covered other typical toddler behaviors so she could understand Melody better and have realistic expectations of her. I encouraged Tiffany to improve her parenting and discipline skills by taking a parenting class and gave her resources to get started. I suggested that Tiffany play more with Melody to strengthen their bond and emotional connection, which would increase adherence. I convinced her to focus on the wonderful things Melody was doing, such as when she briefly sat quietly on the floor or when she played nicely with the toys. Most of what was perceived as misbehavior could be ignored, and only a few things needed intervention. Tiffany was very receptive. So we practiced several times when they came into the clinic, and Tiffany's use of "No, stop, don't . . ." decreased.

Parents can mold child behavior toward what they want to see when they encourage positive behavior, say things in the right way, lead by example, and motivate their kids to choose wisely. Try these strategies out. You may find this difficult to do initially, because even adults have trouble changing habits. Research suggests it takes 66 days, or more than 2 months, to form a new habit. So expect the same with you and your kids. Give your kids time in allowing them to change or form positive behavior. Be patient but consistent. And remember to keep it peaceful and positive!

4. Discouraging and Correcting Negative Behavior

Although most of our time should be spent by encouraging positive behavior, kids are going to do some things wrong, requiring us to have skills in managing misbehavior like "loud house" stuff, sibling fights, meltdowns, not following the rules, lying, and talking back. Ask yourself the following questions before responding to misbehavior:

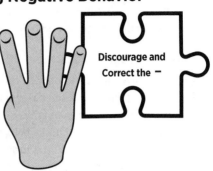

Discourage and Correct the −

- Is this behavior appropriate for the child's developmental stage? If the answer is yes, technically the child is not misbehaving. However, the behavior may be unwanted. Be patient and continue to show and teach the child the right way.
- What is this behavior trying to communicate? Is the child tired, hungry, bored, scared, or seeking attention? Meet the need, and the behavior will likely resolve.
- Is this behavior potentially harmful or unkind? If not, you may not need to intervene at all. Little deal. If so, planning how you want to handle big deal or "deal breaker" behavior is important.
- Is what you're about to do or say positive and helpful to your child? Kids can definitely do some things that trigger us emotionally. But we can't hold them responsible for our actions. We control what we do and say to our kids.

Take about 10 seconds to really process the child's behavior before responding. This 10-second rule allows you to seek understanding first, decide the severity of the behavior, and calm down and think of a positive response or solution. Ten seconds can make all the difference.

Oftentimes when parents explain home life dynamics to me, I find that they expect the impossible. Toddlerhood is a perfect example of this expectation when parents find it hard to accept typical toddler behaviors—hitting, biting, tantrums, lots of energy, and very little focus.

Also, caregivers tend to focus on stopping the behavior, rather than the reason the child is behaving that way. A classic example of this tendency is when caregivers don't realize that children are tired or hungry. Just like adults, they become irritable, "hangry" even, and are more likely to act out. Understanding this behavior as it occurs is key to managing the behavior appropriately. Get the child something to eat, help them go to sleep, and comfort them. Their behavior isn't intentional or mean-spirited; rather, it's just a symptom of a problem the parents should recognize and help solve.

First, Pick Your Battles

You don't have enough energy or time in a day to correct everything your child does wrong. Generally, I tell parents to work on behaviors that are harmful and unkind—you know, unacceptable, deal breaker stuff—and as the parent, you get to decide what those are. Unsafe behaviors put lives in danger or can cause serious injury. These include putting a fork into an electrical outlet, jumping from the top of the stairs, throwing a glass, hitting, texting while driving, and using drugs. Unkind behaviors are emotionally hurtful and potentially damage the overall success of the child within society. These include name-calling, bullying, excluding others, not sharing, and spreading rumors. It seems that kids also lack manners these days (OK, boomer), but manners really matter. So correcting behaviors that undermine your values, morals, and beliefs is worth striving for. These include not saying please, thank you, yes, no, or, if you're in the South, yes ma'am or no ma'am.

Remember, you should spend most of your time by focusing on the good things your kids are doing. Some research suggests giving 10 to 15 praises for every correction. Then correct behaviors that are unsafe and unkind. The other, minor infractions or unwanted behaviors can be managed more naturally and tend to work themselves out, because they are likely phases. For instance, think of when a baby keeps dropping their sippy cup on the floor and cries for you to pick it up or think back to when Brian arrived at camp with only one shoe on. Yes, these are nerve-racking, messy, and inconvenient, but, in all honesty, a "little deal" in the grand scheme of things. Kids learn to do better by watching us, interacting with others, maturing, and being appropriately disciplined. So let's get into some ways to support them and manage the things they do.

Attention

Parents, teachers, and other caregivers, your attention is a superpower! (Another pearl I learned in parenting class.) Deciding when to give it or remove it is critical in dealing with child behavior. We've discussed how kids love and need our attention. Giving attention is loving, supportive, and a good way to connect with your child. It sends the message "Yay, do more of that!" So if you notice your son comforting his little sister and you say, "Such a kind big brother," he will likely try being kind more. Positive reinforcement. On the other hand, if you keep picking up the cup for your baby (giving your attention to the unwanted behavior), you will find yourself stuck in a cycle of up-down. If dropping the cup was an accident, by all means pick it up. But when it becomes repetitive, the child is most likely finished with the cup, so you should remove it from the area. And ignore the crying that ensues or try the next puzzle piece in this chapter—redirection and distraction. See how that works?

When we pay attention to misbehavior (unless it is unsafe or unkind), we can escalate the behavior, because we pay attention to it. Often kids misbehave because they're searching for attention and connection, so use this knowledge to your advantage. Removing your attention or ignoring a misbehavior is an effective skill to manage child behavior. To ignore a behavior you don't want to happen, turn away. It fades, because the child gets nothing from it. So water the plant, not the weeds. If Johnny tries to run into the street or eat a Tide laundry detergent pod, by all means speak loudly and forcefully and pick him up immediately. But if Bailey whines a lot, popping in your earbuds or walking away until she uses her words will teach her a better way to communicate. For younger children, suggesting the right words or saying "I don't understand you, can you use your words?" may be helpful as well. Choose wisely. Know when to give your attention and when to withhold it.

Redirection and Distraction

My visit with Tiffany and Melody is a great example of when to redirect and distract. You probably recall that Melody was super busy in the examination room, which is typical of a toddler. However, she was doing some things that were unsafe, like playing in the trash can and opening the cabinets. I'm thinking lots of germs and smashed fingers. So I advised Tiffany to redirect and distract Melody from those behaviors. For instance, Tiffany could have played a game of Simon Says and sung nursery rhymes like "Head, Shoulders, Knees, and Toes" with Melody while they waited in the exam room. When Melody got into trouble by opening the trash can, Tiffany could have directed her attention to something acceptable, like coloring or reading together. For example, "The trash can is yucky. Let's color the puppy dog." (It helps if you act like a puppy dog.) This skill can be used repeatedly and works every time!

Coaching Cues

We mentioned earlier how discipline is all about teaching kids and the goal is for kids to not only behave but gain the ability to make positive choices for themselves. Various verbal and nonverbal prompts work to cue appropriate behavior. They help children gain impulse control, critical thinking, and decision-making skills— all skills kids need to leave the nest and soar on their own. Consistent prompting also conditions children to accept being corrected without all the back and forth.

Using prompts reminds me of coaching. Coaches stand on the sideline and direct their players to success. They don't play in the game, but their short, clear, and concise prompts are valuable for victory. "Blue!" cues the right play. "Backdoor!" signals the defense to watch for an opponent sneaking to get open. An emphatic handclap or fist pump boosts team morale and keeps up the energy. And just a look and nod communicate "You got this" or "Go for it."

Verbal Prompts

A popular verbal prompt for child misbehavior is to ask a thought-provoking question, such as "Is that a good choice?" Most children will pause and at least think about it, leaving the perfect opportunity to teach or show better options. Be prepared for some children to be mischievous and say, "Yes!" In that case, I usually respond, "Are you sure? I don't think so," or "No, that's not a good choice." Also, younger children may not fully understand the concepts of yes/no or right/wrong, so their "Yes" may be innocent. Just keep working at prompting. They will get it eventually.

Another favorite verbal prompt I learned from a mom is "asked and told." It works like a charm when kids keep begging you for something they want. You know, the "Please mom . . . but I just want . . . why can't I . . . ?" Saying "asked and told" communicates to the child, you asked, I listened, I decided, I will not change my mind, and now we're moving on. Don't argue back and forth with kids!

Probably one of the most frustrating things for parents is when their kids don't follow instructions or listen right away. As parents, we expect that when we say to do something, our kids will. To have to repeat ourselves again and again can be stressful. In this situation, first get your child's full attention. They should be looking directly at you and not engaged with whatever they were doing previously. Give them clear instructions, one step at a time; have them repeat the instructions back to you; and give them a few seconds to get started. Most kids will respond nicely. However, for those who don't, counting down can kick-start adherence. I use 5- or 10-second countdowns depending on the task and the age of the child (or use a timer for a longer task).

For example, when I ask my daughter to come and eat or get dressed, she sometimes says, "No," or "I don't want to." Then, I say, "Yes, please," or "But I want you to." She usually follows at this point, but if she doesn't, I count down: "5, 4, 3, 2, 1." And there she goes, running to her room or to the kitchen table. If not, I pick her up and bring her to the table to eat or to her room to get dressed. Once the countdown starts, she jumps into action, because she knows, at this point, I will have her do it anyway. The key is, you have to follow through once you apply the countdown or it won't work at all. "The countdown is the cue, the follow-through is the do."

Nonverbal Prompts

Nonverbal prompts are also amazing. For example, teaching baby sign language to older infants enhances communication between the parent and child well before words are formed. This can lessen tantrums because the child is able to communicate certain needs and wants. You probably recognize the phrase "If I were you. . . ." You know, that glare that says "Mom is *not* happy right now." Or the face you give your child that says "I am being serious!" I have this blank, deer in the headlights stare that brings my toddler to laughter (and adherence), and my son stops whatever he is doing and shrugs his shoulders, as if to say, "What?" My laser stare means "Not the right choice" or "This calls for consequences." A shake of the head no or yes, a "come here" finger, a 5-finger stop sign, or a pat on a chair signaling for them to sit down are all just as powerful as our words, if not more. Because sometimes we just talk too much. So add a few nonverbal prompt pieces to help solve your discipline puzzle. The possibilities are endless when it comes to using prompts to manage behavior. Create your own—the art of discipline!

To master the skill of verbal and nonverbal prompts, you must project a nurturing but firm response. A nurturing voice sounds loving, kind, and sort of singsong. Not the "mean voice" my son so eloquently describes. Believe it or not, children can tell the difference. And the tone or intent of your voice influences how they choose to behave. When we respond in a mean way, they will too and are less likely to follow our instructions. When we are nurturing, they melt like butter. Similarly, a firm voice captures attention and communicates that you're in charge and unwavering in what you are asking them to do. Children understand that this is nonnegotiable and you mean business. *Nurturing* and *firm* may sound like polar opposites, but they work beautifully together, like yin and yang.

Tell a Story, Sing a Song (The More Childlike, the Better)

Telling stories is also effective to impart behavioral wisdom and practice decision-making. Now these don't have to be long-drawn-out stories that make children regret the day they were born. For instance, when your preschooler gets into trouble at school for taking toys away from their friends, using a story or character from a book or show they watch, like Swiper the Fox in *Dora the Explorer,* may help explain the importance of asking for a turn nicely and being a good friend.

There are also wonderful songs that can help discourage misbehavior. My daughter surprised me with one recently. She sang Daniel Tiger's song proudly, "It's OK to feel angry. It's not, not, not OK to hurt someone." When she hits or throws something, I sing it back to her and she seems to get it. PBS Kids and *Sesame Street* show children how to manage their emotions and behave appropriately through amazing content. You should watch with your child and use the stories and songs to modify behavior.

Avoid Harsh Punishment

Behavior analyst Glenn Latham, PhD, states in his book *The Power of Positive Parenting* that "if the behavior gets weaker, or stops, then it has been punished." To punish a behavior is to decrease the behavior. When your child misbehaves and you punish them, are you really giving a punishment? Did the behavior decrease? Did it continue or increase? You may think you gave a punishment, but you may have increased the unwanted behavior. I often see parents hitting or yelling at their child for crying, and in most cases, it won't decrease the crying but instead can fuel it.

Also, how you deliver punishment is equally as important. If you punish punitively or with ill intent, you can cause harm and you risk creating more problem behaviors (eg, if, after your child gets suspended for cheating on a test, you spank him with a belt and say, "You are an embarrassment. Stay in your room forever—don't come out except to eat or go to the bathroom. And give me your phone, TV, and game console. Bet you won't do that again!").

This is an example of harsh punishment, and it has long-term negative effects on your child. It can weaken trust, evoke shame and anger, and brew resentment and rebellion. It also undercuts the parent-child relationship as the child finds ways to avoid being harshly punished by lying and hiding—breeding more misbehavior. Additionally, it sends the message to your child that they are a bad person who deserves to be hurt.

As a pediatrician, I encourage parents to carefully use punishment to decrease behavior in a way that is nonpunitive, non-retaliatory, instructive, and restorative. In the prior example, the child had already received a punishment that would have likely ensured he never cheat again—suspension from school. The parent could have added punishment by having the child restudy for the test and retake it as well as by creating the space for the child to express why he cheated and how to prevent doing so in the future.

Consequences

Positive discipline, a concept based on the initial work of Alfred Adler to the present-day work of Jane Nelsen, EdD, focuses on various types of consequences to modify behavior.

All of your actions in response to your child's behavior, whether positive or negative, are consequences. A smile when they clean up the mess they made is positive. Calling them "messy" is negative. But for this section to focus on managing misbehavior, the skill of applying consequences is described as the response or action that follows an unwanted behavior. Somewhere during science, we all learned that for every action, there is an equal and opposite reaction. Well, the same applies in discipline—actions have reactions, or consequences. In positive discipline, consequences are given in a nurturing and connected way, and the goal is to foster self-discipline and problem-solving in the child (and not to be punitive or hurtful)—for example, a parent saying to their child, "You still haven't cleaned your room. What are we going to do about it?" When children offer solutions to their own problems, they are more likely to choose better next time. This helps children consider their actions and how those affect others as well as teaches responsibility, accountability, and even empathy.

Rules of Using Consequences

For consequences to be an effective disciplinary strategy, and a piece in the positive parenting puzzle, they must be given correctly. Here are some guidelines for using them in the right way.

- Consequences should be given in a positive and peaceful manner. Practice the 10-second rule. Calm down and think before you give the consequence. You don't have to rush into it.
- Make sure the consequence is fair or matches the severity of the misbehavior.
- Give your child a chance. Clearly explain what the consequence will be for the unwanted behavior. If your child does it anyway or does it again, apply the consequence.
- Speak in a nurturing, yet firm way.
- Explain to your child what they did wrong and give better solutions. Talk the behavior and solutions out with them. To make sure your child understands, ask them what better choices they would make next time.
- Avoid consequences that cause pain or shame.
- Do what you say you're going to do. Follow through with the consequence.
- Be consistent. Don't give a consequence for hitting today and let it slide tomorrow. And share how you give consequences with other caregivers to ensure consistency.
- Consequences should be given for a period of time based on the age of the child. Young children don't remember consequences given over a long period. And of course, neither do you.
- Don't overuse any specific type of consequence; change it up a little and get creative.
- Never take away necessities—for example, food, water, shelter, or safety.

Types of Consequences

1. **Natural consequences** happen on their own, without any help from you. Let's say experience is the best teacher. If your daughter throws and breaks

her toy, she will be unable to play with it and she will soon learn to be gentler with her toys. If your son keeps forgetting to take his homework to school, failing the assignment might help him remember to complete his homework next time. And if your teenager spends all of her money on a new pair of shoes, she will miss out on her weekly Starbucks Frappuccino.

2. **Logical consequences** are created by you and related to the misbehavior. When your daughter throws a toy, you could take the toy away for a period of time. For the son who can't seem to remember to take his homework to school, having him create a morning checklist might solve the problem. And for your adolescent who is spending money unwisely, helping her create a budget is key.

3. **Removal of privileges** isn't natural or may not be related to the behavior. It can be used when there are multiple, repeated, or severe misbehaviors. The purpose is to remove something of value to the child in hopes that they will behave better to regain the privilege. For instance, if your child had a rough day at school—talking in class and refusing to do work—you might restrict electronic or TV time until your child behaves appropriately at school.

4. **Time-out** has become a controversial disciplinary tool because it is often done wrong and overused. Some experts believe that time-outs do little to help children learn to regulate their emotions. However, when used effectively, a time-out can be an appropriate consequence to curb unwanted behavior. So take the time to do it correctly.

   You will need a place for your child to stay in time-out. It should be located away from the attention of others and free of stimulating things. The child can stand in time-out, but a chair or mat is better to set the boundaries of the time-out space. If you have difficulty keeping your child in the designated space or you are not at home, feel free to improvise by using a quiet bedroom, or dressing room in a store, or quick trip to the car.

   If your child misbehaves and you decide a time-out is needed, follow these simple steps to do it correctly.

   Correct the behavior and give your child a time-out warning.

   Ask your child, "Do we hit? Keep your hands to yourself. The next time you hit, you will go to time-out." If the child follows instructions, make sure to praise them. If they hit again, a time-out is warranted. And remember to follow through on what you said you would do. Sometimes a warning is impossible. For example, a child who is throwing a tantrum may need to be taken to time-out right away until they calm down.

   Explain the reason for the time-out.

   "You hit again. Go to time-out." Use a nurturing but firm voice. No lecturing or arguing back and forth. No repeating yourself. Don't allow bargaining to get out of the consequence or third chances. Remove your attention and direct or take your child to their time-out space.

Call time-out.

Your child may refuse to go to or stay in time-out initially. You may have to sit there with them, hold them in place, or keep putting them back. Warning! Kids may headbutt, kick, or scream at the top of their lungs in the beginning, but remember to keep your cool and try not to talk to your child during the process. I promise, it will get better with time.

Set a timer and give 1 minute of time-out per year of age (adjust this for how long your child is able to sit developmentally).

- Two years old = 2 minutes.
- Three years old = 3 minutes.
- Four years old = 4 minutes.
- Five years old = 5 minutes.

Time-out can be effective for older children and teens as well: "Take a time-out to think about what you've done and we'll talk later" or "Go take a time-out until you are calm and ready to talk respectfully." This creates a break for both the parent and child to think, manage emotions, and practice self-control. Even adults can take a time-out.

In the case of 2 or more children misbehaving or acting out of control, feel free to call a time-out for everyone. Just make sure to send them to separate spaces, and then the same steps apply.

"You can come out now."

Let your child out of time-out when they are calm and the time is complete. If they aren't calm, you can remind them that they must calm down to end the time-out. Listen for a brief period of quiet, then let them out. At this point, feel free to talk to your child about what they did wrong and what you expect from them. If your child was in time-out for not adhering to your request, repeat the instructions and hopefully your child will do what you asked this time. If not, back to time-out. It may take several trips to the time-out space before your child understands you mean what you say.

Also, instead of a time-out, you can use a positive parenting tool called "time in." For example, Sarah is having a meltdown. Instead of using a time-out, her grandmother asks her to come closer and cuddle, helping her calm quickly. Then she and her grandmother discuss why she got so upset and how to use her words to express her feelings next time. This not only addresses the unwanted behavior but also promotes connection, empathy, and problem-solving skills.

5. Managing the Environment

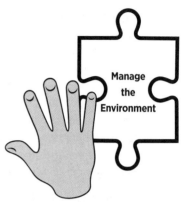

The fifth and final essential piece of the positive parenting puzzle is Managing the Environment. Remember, you can't control how your child chooses to behave, but you can control yourself and the environment. You can anticipate problems and plan the environment, adjust the environment, and remove your family from any environment that is not conducive to positive behavior. That's CEO-level stuff right there! Being a parent is upper-level management and much more. You not only lead from the top but also supervise your little workers and even get in the trenches, working alongside them, to ensure the success of your family.

Failing to manage your family's environment leaves you reacting to things your children do or don't do. In this situation, you're already at a disciplinary disadvantage and playing catch-up to help your child behave. This is when emotions can get the best of you—frustration, anger, a sense of being overwhelmed and outright tired of . . . the struggle is real! So stop playing catch-up and reacting. Go on offense.

To set your kids up for successful behavior, you need to

Be Proactive, Not Reactive

Being proactive guides children toward positive choices. This requires planning, anticipating, and being creative on the caregiver's part. **Planning** prevents problems. For example, prepping the night before, using a morning checklist, and getting up a little bit earlier can help you prevent running extremely late. Just think of all the drama your family can avoid.

Anticipating prepares you to stay one step ahead of your child. To foresee what your child will do, you have to know them well and what's typical for them developmentally. If you have a very busy toddler like Melody, anticipating how they'll respond to being cooped up in a small examination room for nearly an hour is very important in keeping them out of trouble. Anticipate their playing in the garbage can and cabinets. They're toddlers after all and probably do that at home. Sit in front of the object or distract them with some of their favorite toys when they head in that direction. Again, bring snacks, just in case they get hungry, and their comfort blanket or doll, just in case they need to nap. On the other hand, if you're on Instagram, not supervising your child or engaging them while you wait, they'll likely misbehave. Then all you can do is react like Tiffany did.

As a pediatrician, I enjoy giving anticipatory guidance to parents. I explain that toddlers will throw a tantrum, bite, or hit and I offer ways to prevent and handle these behaviors appropriately. I prepare parents of school-aged children about lying and disobedience. And for the rebellious, hormonal teen years, I advise parents on how to support their teen along the bumpy ride.

Last, **getting creative** requires finding solutions that will discourage misbehavior in your child. Several examples were given to help Melody behave well in the exam room. For older children and teens, tools like the family media use plan, parental control apps, and driving notifications to prevent texting help keep kids on the straight and narrow.

Although some things can't be planned or anticipated, thinking forward as much as possible sets your family up for behavioral success and is a strong piece of the discipline puzzle.

Establish Structure and Routines

Setting up a structured environment and keeping routines are like kryptonite to the chaos that kids can bring. Kids need structure and routines because they don't know what to do, and when left to their own devices, they often make poor choices. So it's our job to create an environment that guides them throughout the day to keep them safe, meet their basic needs, and support their optimal development. As children grow, they also need to learn how to care for themselves. Establishing routines within a structured environment helps them build executive function skills and become more independent. Routines train positive behaviors. You see, structure and routines work together.

A sample school day could follow a checklist.

- Wake-up routine: Brush your teeth, wash your face, make your bed, eat breakfast.
- After-school routine: Put your backpack and shoes where they go, wash your hands, change your clothes, eat snacks, freely play/relax, practice piano, start your homework.
- Dinnertime: Eat at the table with family (electronic-free), take your plates over to the sink and either wash them off or put them into the dishwasher.
- Bedtime: Set a time, take a shower, have quiet time (electronic-free) or read a book in bed, lights out.

Set Limits and Rules

By setting limits and rules, parents teach kids self-discipline and how to make positive behavioral choices. Children learn through rules what's expected of them and how to think in a well-ordered way. Setting limits and rules also helps them feel safe and secure. Doing so is not being tough on your kids. It's being a great parent by preparing them for relationships, school, a career, and just about anything else in life. In fact, a lack of limits and rules breeds negative behavior and poor self-control in kids. So let's talk about how to make rules so your kids are more likely to follow them.

Making Family Rules

1. Make sure the rule is developmentally appropriate for the child; otherwise, you are setting your child up for failure and trouble. Can they do it? Rules can be modified as the child develops. Also, each child within the home may have different rules based on abilities.
2. Explain the rule. Be clear and simple. Don't assume your child understands anything.
3. Answer any questions your child may have.
4. Have your child repeat the rule.
5. Inform your child that there are consequences for breaking rules.
6. Consistently enforce the rule and apply consequences.
7. Post deal breaker rules around the house for review and as reminders.

You can set limits and rules about anything. House rules. Going out to eat rules. School rules. And so forth. But don't go overboard; too many rules will be difficult for both you and your kids to remember. So really think about what rules are important to you. Rules regarding manners, conduct, values and beliefs, household duties, education, and health/hygiene are all fair.

You and your kids could work on a fun family activity together by creating a house rules list like the following one:

Family House Rules

Health	Shower, brush your teeth, apply deodorant daily, turn off all devices at bedtime
Household	Make your bed, clean your room, take out the trash, ask for permission to eat or for that to play electronics
Conduct	Be kind, keep your hands to yourself
Education	Read, practice math and piano daily, finish your homework, limit electronics during the school week
Manners, values, and beliefs	Be respectful of adults, accept others, pray before meals and bedtime

You can reinforce rules by giving verbal prompts, creating checklists, and, as a last resort, giving consequences. For example, if you notice your son watching TV around bedtime, you can say, "It's bedtime, what's the rule?" or "It's bedtime, where are you on the checklist?" or "What do we do at bedtime? That's right, so turn the TV off." And don't forget to use your nurturing, firm, singsong voice.

You can also coach your kids regarding boundaries before an outing or special event by going over the rules.

> **Dad:** OK, Keisha, what's the rule when we're in the mall?
>
> **Keisha:** We stay with Mommy and Daddy.
>
> **Mom:** James, do we touch and pick up things in the store?
>
> **James:** No, because they might break. But can I ask if it's OK to pick something up?
>
> **Mom:** Yes, then I can tell you if you can pick it up.
>
> **Dad:** What do we do when we get in the restaurant?
>
> **Kids:** Sit in our seat.
>
> **Dad:** Good job—see, you guys already know what to do.

Thou Shalt Not Tempt a Child

If you leave medications or markers where curious toddlers can get them, best believe you'll be calling Poison Control or spending hours cleaning your favorite chair. Don't expect to be successful at keeping a child from eating junk food when you have cakes, candies, and chips out in the open or readily accessible for them to eat. Most adults find it hard to resist junk food, so of course children do too. The impulse to eat it is just too hard to resist. With childhood obesity at epidemic proportions, I advise parents not to bring junk food home or at least to secure it from their child only to be given at parental discretion. Another common temptation is electronics. It's much easier to collect all devices and remotes at bedtime than to find your child breaking the rule at 2:00 am and have to figure out a consequence. Teens, especially, aren't happy about this, but they won't be tempted to break a rule and will get the sleep they need to be happier and healthier. Sorry, not sorry.

Kids will break rules and test limits. Pushing boundaries for kids is typical. Reinforcing your rules and giving consequences for breaking them is typical as well. That's your job as a parent, and doing so is important for your child to learn and behave at home and in life.

Give Choices

When you give children choices, they practice decision-making skills. This helps them feel more independent, which will boost their self-confidence. Choices also help children gain self-control and learn consequences. As a parent, you have the responsibility to send the right message. I trust you'll make the best decision.

Kids cooperate better when given choices. This gives them a sense of power. If your son is always yelling, "No, I don't want that!" at dinner, try giving him a few choices and watch him smile at being able to choose. You can say, "David, would you like green beans or corn with your chicken?" And maybe your daughter is pouting at bedtime simply because she didn't get to choose her pajamas or a stuffed animal to sleep with. The beauty of this approach is that you set the boundary. Limit it to 2 or 3 choices, so the child isn't overwhelmed. They get to choose. No power struggle. No yelling. No controlling or forcing the issue. And everybody wins.

Now that the essential pieces of discipline have been connected, is the puzzle becoming clearer? I hope so. There are a few more pieces to connect before we solve this puzzle, so just keep reading. But note here that Knowledge of Child Development and Parenting Skills serves as the foundation of child development and behavior. If the parental foundation is weak, everything else is unstable, including your child's behavior. The other essential pieces, Good Relational Health Between Parent and Child, Encouraging Positive Behavior, and Managing the Environment, should be used freely and often to encourage desired behavior. Then the piece used to handle misbehavior (Discouraging and Correcting Negative Behavior) won't be necessary as often, becoming an even more powerful tool in your disciplinary skill set.

I challenge you to take a long, hard look at your current discipline approach. Is it working? Is it hurting? May I suggest that you chip away the negative, ineffective pieces and replace them with some of the pieces mentioned in this chapter. They work and they don't hurt. A win-win approach! You get to choose what you think will work for your child and family. Start developing your family positive parenting plan today (see Chapter 12, Piecing Together a Plan, for a template and a sample).

Parenting Prescription

Start to create your own family discipline plan. Highlight strategies from each essential piece that you think may work for your child. Chapter 12, Piecing Together a Plan, has a template and a sample.

PART 3

Adult in the Mirror

You must be the change you wish to see in the world.

—Mahatma Gandhi

Chapter 3

Selfies

As I tried on shoes in front of the mirror in T.J. Maxx, I could hear in the distance a very loud, harsh voice saying, "Stop it! Get over here! If you touch one more thing, I'm gonna pop you!" As they walked down the aisle in my direction, I could see the mom grab her little girl roughly by the arm and walk fast, as if she were in a hurry. The little girl began to cry. The mom stopped, bent down, and yelled in her girl's face, "Don't start that crying! You just wait until you get home. I'll give you something to cry about!" as she shook her head and pushed her girl toward the door to exit the store.

My heart broke for this child who couldn't have been any more than 3 or 4 years old. I thought about the trauma she must have endured behind closed doors. How maltreatment might become normal to her and how she was likely to repeat these same, harmful behaviors with her children.

Let's be honest. Dealing with kids' behavior can be exhausting, annoying, and overwhelming. They are cute, loving, and funny one minute and outright difficult the next, to say the least. Not to mention, as a responsible adult, you have so much on your plate and on your mind regarding your job, your personal relationships, and your expenses. And then there's always your kids and their after-school activities, their homework, and, oh, their dinner too. Every moment potentially chips away at your ability to keep it all together and maintain a sense of control.

First, take a deep breath and know that you are not alone. All caregivers feel this way at one time or another; this feeling is common. Perhaps the mom in the mall was just having a bad day and had no more cool left in her. Perhaps she hadn't known that treating a child this way is inappropriate. I'd like to think we are all trying to do the best we can. However, if we want to encounter better in this world, we have to start by being better ourselves, as well as being the best parents and role models for our children.

Let's take a few "selfies." And I don't mean the ones you take with your cell phone. I am speaking about the ones that are part of your self-empowerment or self-improvement. Self-esteem, self-confidence, self-respect, and self-worth are all examples. If you take a deeper look at who you are as a parent and how you appear to your children, selfies like self-reflection and self-care are important elements to start with.

Taking "selfies" reminds me of the lyrics "I'm starting with the man in the mirror," because I believe we should always be looking at "self" through a figurative mirror to identify areas we can improve on and to maintain a level of self-awareness at all times. If the mother in the store did "mirror checks," she would see the need to improve her behavior toward her little girl. When you try to see yourself and gain insight into your own behaviors, you may realize there is room for change. "Yes, make that positive change . . . ," parent in the mirror.

Self-reflection

During my parenting class with behavior analyst Tara Concelman, I did an exercise that was so powerful and memorable that I share it with parents all the time. It's an exercise in self-reflection, developed by Richard West, PhD, Utah State University, and explored by Glenn Latham, PhD, in the book *The Power of Positive Parenting*, that will help you examine yourself as a parent.

First think about an authority figure from your childhood who positively influenced your life and write down the leadership traits that helped you grow.

Now do the opposite and write down the characteristics of an authority figure from your childhood who left a negative impression on you and potentially kept you from growing and feeling positive.

Here is the list I made from that day.

Positive (Grow)	Negative (No!)
Funny	Fusses/yells
Patient	Mean/angry
Nurturing	Too serious
Listens	Doesn't listen
Instructive	Impatient
Praises	Irritable
Supportive	Critical

Now, it's your turn! Please take a moment to fill out the following chart with your list of characteristics:

Positive (Grow)	Negative (No!)
_____	_____
_____	_____
_____	_____
_____	_____
_____	_____
_____	_____
_____	_____

I had the opportunity to follow up with Tara about this exercise. On my podcast, *KIDing Around with Dr. Candice*, Tara said, "Oftentimes we discover, in that comparison, the kind of parent we're actually being is the person we wanted to get away from—a reactive parent, a punishing parent. Someone who criticizes and who isn't supportive. We aren't always that way and don't see ourselves that way until we look at our history. Then we realize that we are engaging in some of those same behaviors." You see, we may not even realize that we've adopted some of the same "bad" parenting habits from our childhood. We've become the very thing we despise or didn't want to be. Now, can you imagine how our children feel.

This exercise made me think back fondly to times with my grandmother and some of my favorite teachers, Mr Mills and Coach Softley, when I was reflecting on my best adult encounters as a child and teenager. On the other hand, I had to shake off the visuals of certain grown-ups, who I wished I had never met. I knew for certain that I didn't want to be *those* people, *those* memories, in the life of any child, especially not my own.

You'll identify your parenting strengths and weaknesses by doing this exercise just as I did. Through this exercise, you should be striving to become the parent you always wanted to have. That "grow" parent, teacher, or other caregiver who's kind, supportive, patient, funny, understanding, instructive, a good listener, and more. Someone you look up to and can depend on. Knowing these traits about yourself is the first step in becoming the parent that your children will treasure and blossom under.

All child caregivers need to do this exercise as well. No adult or child is perfect. We should all love ourselves unconditionally, accepting the good, the bad, and the ugly. But we should make room for positively growing in our personal lives and, as a parent, improving on the relationships and interactions with our kids.

This is the human experience or "parenting experience." We bounce between Grow and No! behaviors. When things are great, we are the best, but when things are tough, we sometimes default to knee-jerk responses that we aren't proud of. Knowing where you naturally fall short gives you the power to pause when the heat is rising and before you boil over. Then you can choose your response carefully, so no harm is done.

After you self-reflect, share your list with a close friend, with a significant other, or even with your older children. Ask them, "Where do you think I am on this list, and where would you like me to be?" Like me, you probably straddle both sides and that's OK. Don't be defensive about the feedback you receive. This truth might be hard for your child to tell, so be positive. Take it all in and keep an open mind.

This exercise is about you as a parent learning more about yourself and how you interact with your children to improve your relationship. You may find that you often blame your kids but, in all honesty, you are to blame too and actually add fuel to the fire. Instead of co-escalating, you need to find ways to co-regulate with your kids. The traits you discover that discourage or frustrate your children only need to go on your "room for improvement" (No!) list. According to my son Miles, I am "mostly positive, with a little fussiness and impatience."

Yeah, so I am working on that!

Self-care

I'm sure most of you have heard of the oxygen masks on an airplane analogy: their proper use can be parallel to the importance of self-care. We've all been there. The flight attendant says, "In the event of an emergency, oxygen masks will drop down from the ceiling. Put your mask on your face first, and then assist others, including small children." Then another attendant walks around to remind adults with children to place their mask on first and then help their children. Everyone would agree that it would be natural to help our children first and worry about ourselves later.

But what would happen to your child if you perished from a lack of oxygen? It makes sense to ensure that we have enough oxygen first in order to help our children and be there for them for the long haul. You could replace *oxygen* with any word that describes your needs, including your own emotional, mental, and physical well-being, that should be addressed before you can be fully capable of helping and guiding your own child.

Again, self-care is not selfish! It's actually selfless, because caring for yourself greatly benefits others around you, especially your kids. People also view self-care as a luxury when, actually, it should be viewed as a necessity or prioritized toward living our best lives. So don't feel guilty when you choose to care for your mental, physical, and spiritual selves.

You can give only what you have. How can you fill your child's cup if your cup is empty? Individuals who grew up neglected, lacking love and connection, may find it difficult to emotionally support their spouse, children, or friends. Some adults who experienced sexual abuse in childhood shy away from physical acts of affection with their family, like hugging and kissing. And those who had a parent or other caregiver struggling with mental illness or substance use problems have increased risk for those issues themselves. Our past, present, and future are connected. Healing the past, addressing present concerns, and planning for a better future are all important self-care goals.

Therefore, as parents, developing and maintaining a **self-care plan,** to address your physical, psychological, emotional, spiritual, professional, and social needs, is a good starting point.

Caring for Yourself Physically

All parents should have regular health checkups to prevent disease, maintain health, and manage health conditions. Prioritize living a healthy lifestyle for not only you but your entire family. You should eat fruits, vegetables, whole grains, and lean meats and drink plenty of water. Try to limit processed and sugary foods.

Unfortunately, during this year of the COVID-19 pandemic (2019), nearly 1 in 4 households has experienced food insecurity, according to the US Department of Agriculture. And poor communities and communities of color are disproportionately located in food deserts, where finding affordable, quality, healthful foods is very challenging.

Avoid smoking, excessive alcohol intake, and illicit drugs. Exercise at least 3 days or 150 minutes a week. Did you know that a lack of sleep greatly affects mood, learning, stress levels, weight, and so much more? All of these health-promoting activities will keep your body in tip-top shape, ready to keep up with your busy kids or whatever you need it to do.

Sleeping Tips

- ► Keep a bedtime routine, and try to get at least 8 hours of sleep each night.
- ► Limit naps to 30 minutes.
- ► Set a specific bedtime for yourself.
- ► Limit caffeine intake and eating at bedtime.
- ► Turn off screens at least an hour before bedtime.
- ► Read a book.
- ► Listen to relaxing music, or drink chamomile tea.
- ► Talk with your doctor if you have trouble sleeping.

Caring for Yourself Psychologically

The body and mind are connected. If one fails, the other suffers alongside it. So you should pay just as much attention to your mental health as your physical health. When we develop an ear infection, we go to the doctor so they can prescribe an antibiotic, and we take the medication to heal the infection. But the stigma around mental illness deters many from seeking the care they need to address mental and emotional concerns, trapping them in a cycle of dysfunction that hurts everyone and everything around them. If necessary, seek help for yourself and for your children because they need a parent who is mentally well.

As a parent, you have a lot of responsibilities. If you are feeling off, talk with your doctor or find a therapist to help develop a plan to become mentally well. Therapy is a powerful tool to improve mental health by identifying problems and setting goals to solve them. It can help you address many challenges in your life—anxiety, depression, anger, unhealthy relationships, or habits that threaten your mental health and the well-being of your children. It's also very effective in helping manage emotions.

Sometimes you may need to visit with a psychiatrist or other doctor who specializes in diagnosing and treating mental disorders and consider medications to stabilize your mental health (remember that ear infection). This can be temporary but necessary to get you on the right track. Be open to doing whatever it takes to improve your mental health—yes, prayer included. But multiple strategies can help, not just one.

Having a positive mindset is also important when caring for yourself mentally. For example, instead of being concerned about all the things that went wrong today, be intentional about focusing on what went right. For parents who come to me with a laundry list of problems they want to fix about their kid, I often ask, "Tell me what she does well," or "Tell me some things you like about him." This exercise quickly changes the mindset of the parents so they perceive their child in a positive light with a few things to work on, because we all have room for improvement. Keeping your thoughts and your words positive reduces stress, elevates mood, helps you cope better through life challenges, and allows you to perceive things as they really are.

In addition, be careful what you're exposing your mind to. If you spend most of your time watching reality TV, scrolling through social media, or gaming, more important things in your life will become neglected and your thoughts and behaviors may suffer. Take time to learn new things, read, and explore areas that are beneficial to you and your family.

Caring for Yourself Emotionally

The ability to identify, communicate, and manage your emotions and understand the feelings of others is foundational to emotional health. This is referred to as *emotional intelligence* (EI). Individuals vary in levels of EI, from low to high. No matter where you are on the spectrum, you can learn skills to improve EI, which has been shown to benefit parenting, interpersonal skills, and overall success in life. It can certainly help control emotions when one is disciplining children, increasing the likelihood of using positive parenting.

Here are some tips on how to raise your EI.

- Name your emotions and express them openly.
- Allow others to do the same.
- Try to understand the feelings of others.
- In stressful situations, it is important to step away and collect your thoughts and give yourself time to calm down.
- Once you are calm, respond in a helpful way.
- Ask for what you need or want.
- Listen to what others need or want.
- Compromise or take time to think.

For example, a mom says to her teen daughter, "I feel angry when you talk to me that way. I know you're upset over losing phone privileges, but speak to me with respect. If you can't, we'll end this conversation and try again later, when you have calmed down."

Or when a school-aged boy drops his iPad and breaks it, his dad takes a moment to calm down and then says, "I know that was an accident, but I'm upset that your iPad is ruined because you took it out of the case when I told you not too. I know you're upset too, and I hope you've learned a lesson to keep the case on in the future."

In Chapter 10, Be Aware: From ACEs to Healing, we'll discover how stress can help in small, short-lived doses. But when stress is chronic and unbuffered, it can do some real damage and lead to serious health problems. No one is exempt from experiencing stress, so it's wise for us to build our stress management skills. We've already covered some. Sleep, diet, and exercise help the body recover and reduce stress. Therapy can offer effective strategies to manage the emotional response to stress. And honing your EI is instrumental in preventing and resolving stressful events.

Here are a few other tried-and-true strategies to help parents manage their stress and make life's challenges easier. Parents should know

- Their triggers and find ways to avoid or work around them
- When to accept that things are out of their control and move on
- How to ask for help and gather support
- When to check their attitude (way of thinking) and strive to be more optimistic
- When something feels overwhelming, how to break it down into small tasks over time
- When to take a break to relax and recharge
- When to ask for help from a counselor, doctor, or religious leader, such as a pastor, priest, or rabbi

Caring for Yourself Spiritually

Spiritual health is recognized by the World Health Organization as the fourth dimension of health and defined as "that part of the individual which reaches out and strives for meaning and purpose in life. It is the intangible 'something' that transcends physiology and psychology." One of my favorite authors, Brené Brown, said in an interview, "Spirituality is a deeply held belief that we are connected to each other by something greater than us. That something greater is rooted in love and belonging." Strong evidence supports the influence that spiritual health has on overall health and well-being.

Did You Know . . . ?

▶ A strong spiritual life reduces mortality.

▶ Spiritual principles, such as faith, forgiveness, and gratitude, build resilience.

▶ Meditation enhances the brain and immune system, regulates emotions, and relieves stress.

▶ Multiple studies highlight the power of prayer—from preventing hypertension to improving postoperative recovery and boosting the immune system.

▶ Yoga reduces inflammation, eases depression and anxiety, and lowers blood pressure.

Derived from *Explore (NY)*. 2011;7(4):234-238; *J Relig Spiritual Soc Work*. 2019;38(1):93-114; *Indian J Psychiatry*. 2009;51(4):247-253; *Int J Psychiatry Med*. 1998;28(2):189-213; and *Evid Based Complement Alternat Med*. 2012;2012:165410.

For some, spirituality is rooted in religion. For others, spiritual practices include doing things that feed their soul, make them feel at peace, or fulfill a sense of purpose. The possibilities are endless—from going to a place of worship to practicing prayer, yoga, meditation, exercise, or the enjoyment of nature to serving others. All can be viewed as spiritual. Whatever you call it, take the time to replenish, relax, or self-indulge, such as during a spa day, to strengthen the spirit and build a better you!

Caring for Yourself Professionally *and* Socially

In these modern times, parents do it all! The old paradigm of one parent staying home, caring for the kids, and another parent being the breadwinner is fading away. Especially because there is a growing number of single-parent households. Modern moms are working moms and business owners and they are climbing the corporate ladder while taking good care of the home. Bringing home the bacon and frying it up in a pan!

For parents to successfully manage work, home, and personal life, they must use a few strategies. It's all about working smart, not necessarily hard. You should

- **Plan and prepare.** As a parent, you should plan your days, weeks, and months by putting everything on a calendar. Use your smartphone or software like Google Calendar, which communicates with your phone. Your calendar will also work well with your kids' after-school activities, parent conferences, pediatrician visits, and dentist appointments. Having these dates on it allows you to be more proactive because you're able to anticipate what's to come and prepare for it.

  According to your calendar, if you know that you have a work presentation at 9:00 am next Tuesday morning, you should prepare. Set aside time each day to complete your presentation well in advance. Procrastination is not your friend! The night before, make sure you lay out your clothes, make your lunch, and set the coffee pot. I've learned that lesson the hard way, after scrambling in the closet the morning of, trying to find something to wear, and being extremely late or looking a hot mess. By talking with your kids the night before, you can explain that you have a meeting in the morning and you can't be late to work. Ask for their help. Kids can pick out their school outfit the night before, pack their backpack, and put their shoes by the door. These little tasks help teach kids organization and help you in the morning too.

  Get up earlier than usual that morning to get yourself ready first and then your kids. Use your verbal prompts and your kids' get-ready checklist and complete a mental checklist yourself to make sure you have everything you need as well. Before you all head out the door, grab an on-the-go breakfast for the ride in the car (maybe Greek yogurt and a banana). See how that works? A drama-free busy morning.

- **Prioritize.** You should have realistic expectations about what you can do, because you just can't do it all. Decide which tasks are most important for the day and complete them one at a time. Don't feel defeated if you get only a couple of things done. It's better than nothing and there's always tomorrow. How do you eat an elephant? One bite at a time! And don't fall into the trap of multitasking if that's not your strong suit. You may find yourself spinning your wheels and getting nothing done instead.

- **Organize.** Having strong organizational skills helps you work more efficiently. Immediately put dates into calendars, with reminders. Create digital and file folders for house-related items, making it easier to come back to them at a later date. In general, assign things a place and put them where they belong. When you are organized, your kids learn to become organized as well. Delegate responsibilities and encourage teamwork with regular check-ins to ensure workflow and to lessen your load. Kids need to know that teamwork makes the dream work! Every child should be assigned responsibilities within the home no matter how minor they are. And tackling projects together such as cooking and cleaning fosters the spirit of family love and support. These skills will help you become more productive and reduce stress at work and home.

- **Learn to say, "Thanks, but no. . . ."** This is an important skill in caring for yourself and your family. Don't overload yourself. Taking on too much is a recipe for disaster that will frustrate and exhaust you. Outside of your mandatory work responsibilities, accept only additional roles as your home and personal life allow. Philanthropy is great, but limit your commitment to efforts aligning with your personal goals. It's OK to say "I'm all booked up right now, check back with me in a few months" or "Although your organization is very important, it's not a good fit for me at this time. Thanks for thinking of me."

- **Know when to get help.** When you work hard at your job yet feel unsupported and unappreciated, you can slide into resentment, anger, and mental and physical distress, which, alone or in combination, can lead to burnout. Recognize these symptoms and find ways to improve your work environment. Consult your professional cabinet to gain clear direction in the matter. Discuss your concerns and needs with the individual or someone in upper management. Use disciplinary action or a formal complaint to communicate seriousness. If nothing improves, it may be time to part ways. Your well-being is much more important. If you are in a demanding, high-stakes career, mental health counseling can be very helpful in managing stress and conflicts that arise professionally.

- **Schedule breaks.** "All work and no play makes" you a dull, bored, unhappy, and tired person. Everyone needs a break and time to let loose and have fun. Sometimes vacationing or changing your role is the refresher you need. Protect your break or lunchtime. That's the time you need to nourish your body, relieve your bladder, handle personal matters, or just escape outside for a little sunshine and fresh air. Especially if you're home with the kids all day. That's a job! You still need a break too. Putting kids on a schedule will allow you to pencil in your break when they nap or to get a little screen time.

- **Strengthen connections.** Be intentional about building and strengthening connections, or those relationships that pour into you. This means setting aside quality time for your significant other, closest friends, and key family members. Take a beauty day with your sister, a night out with the girls, or a weekend getaway with your significant other (make sure to hire a trusted caregiver for your kids). You need it and deserve it. So schedule it and make it happen.

- **Eliminate toxic relationships.** We discussed how maintaining a healthy relationship with your kids is key to positive parenting, but healthy relationships are also integral to self-care. When you are an adult, being in a toxic relationship can negatively affect your health and your kids. Healthy relationships are loving, supportive, nurturing, safe, respectful, and trust-worthy. They are not abusive, selfish, disrespectful, or distrustful.

Exiting an unhealthy relationship can be difficult. But find a way because you deserve better. Love yourself enough to do what's best for you. Once you decide to leave, stick to your decision and give yourself time to heal. Leave safely and put protective measures into place if needed. Seek the support of friends, family, professionals, and community resources.

All of these tips may seem a bit overwhelming, but you probably use some of them already throughout your day. If so, strong work! If not, start to be more intentional about adding in a few of the self-care strategies mentioned. One small change can positively influence your whole life.

Parenting Prescription

Be a "grow" parent and develop your self-care plan.

Self-care Plan: Becoming My Best Self

Please fill in the following sections with ways you can best develop these 5 key areas:

▶ Physical focus: _____

▶ Psychological focus: _____

▶ Emotional focus: _____

▶ Spiritual focus: _____

▶ Professional/social focus: _____

Chapter 4

Top Model

You're always live when it comes to your kids watching you. They have front row seats to your conversations and interactions with others. They are privileged to who you really are, behind closed doors. They watch what you watch on TV and learn your opinions from your phone conversations. They sometimes watch you eat unhealthy foods, while you demand that they eat healthy ones. For most parents, knowing that your kids are watching you is just the thing you need to know to check yourself and model appropriate behavior. But let's be honest, sometimes it isn't that easy being clean. So even though this chapter focuses on the importance of being a positive role model for kids and how to do it, sometimes parents can mess up. I know I have. And it's OK. Even models sometimes fall on the runway. So, do what they did—jump up and keep strutting. And don't forget, your kids are watching. You just have to be more careful next time.

All parents want to raise kind, respectful, honest, and productive kids. One of the most important pieces for making that happen is being a positive role model. It starts with parental self-reflection and making the necessary changes to be your best self. As parents, we are the first and most important example for our children. Our children learn how to care for themselves, love others, handle conflict, and navigate relationships all from watching us.

Have you ever noticed that when your child watches TV, they ask for something they just watched, start to repeat the same phrases they just heard, or mimic the motions of their favorite characters? I giggle when I see my kids behave this way. I have to really watch what I say and do around my 3-year-old toddler. Her behavior is developmentally equivalent to that of a parrot. It drives my son crazy that she constantly copies everything we say or mimics everything we do. And the more inappropriate the words or deeds are, the more likely she is to repeat them. Nothing gets past her. She surprises us with the "Bom bom bi dom bi dum bum bay" from *Truth Hurts* (the Kidz Bop version, of course) and told me the other day to call Mister Sparky, from the TV commercial, when the pantry light wouldn't come on. Admittedly, she reminds me a lot of myself. But it's not just my kids. I see children every day who are acting out the things they see and hear around them, whether from TV, a video game, or individuals in their lives. They are like little sponges, soaking it all up and squeezing it all back out.

As parents, we often subscribe to the saying "I'm a grown-up. You can't do what I do!" or "Do as I say, not as I do!" But in reality, our children will do exactly what we do, say exactly what we say, and act exactly how we act. If we yell, they yell. If we hit, they hit. What do children see when an adult curses the bill collector, hits their spouse, or treats someone unkindly? They copy whatever they see in those situations, no matter what the adult tells them otherwise. In this case, what you do is much more powerful than what you say.

On the other hand, when we demonstrate peace, kindness, patience, positivity, and love, our children will just as easily follow suit. Ultimately, our actions will affect their well-being in every way and influence them to reflect who we are. So as the "parent in the mirror," what you see in the mirror is usually what your children are or will become. Therefore, it's a huge responsibility to be an appropriate and positive role model for our kids.

If you want to be a good parent and a good disciplinarian, you need to be a good top model. Here are some qualities of being a positive role model for your children.

- **Be fair.** Practice the habits you are teaching your child. You set the example for how to do just about everything. Eat healthy if you tell them to. Speak respectfully with your spouse if you're always begging your kids to cut out the sibling rivalry. Don't text while driving if you expect your teenager to drive safely. Hold yourself to your own standards.
- **Be honest.** Tell your kids the truth in a way that is developmentally appropriate for them. For instance, if your family pet dies, you might simply tell your 4-year-old, "I'm so sorry, Fuzzy got hurt and died today." However, you can tell your 10-year-old, "I'm so sorry, Fuzzy ran into the street and got hit by a car. We rushed her to the vet and they did everything they could to save her, but she died of her injuries." Also, don't lie in your kid's presence, because they just might correct you at the wrong time. You know, when they say, "Mom, no we didn't!" in front of their teacher. Talk about em-bar-rass-ing! This discrepancy sends the message to your children that it's OK to lie when it's not.
- **Have strong selfie skills.** When our kids watch us working to be our best selves, whether it's getting that college degree, kicking a habit, or improving our mental and physical health or loving ourselves enough to leave a traumatic relationship, they learn values that will last for a lifetime. Self-improvement at its finest! But self-control is also important. Life gets heated

sometimes and so does home life. So our children need a parent who's in control of themselves to show them how to keep their cool even though flipping their lid is an option. Show your kids that you know how to remain cool, calm, and collected. If you're anxious or easily angered, your kids feel that emotion and are likely to mirror the same behaviors. And don't forget all the other wonderful "selfie" skills you learned about in Chapter 3, Selfies. Modeling selfie skills will ensure that your child has them to use as well.

- **Be kind.** Your kids look up to you. Be careful with how you treat and talk to others in their presence. Your children will either follow your lead or be greatly disappointed in your approach. Teach your kids acts of kindness by giving to those in need, serving in your community, or volunteering for a worthy cause as a family.

    As parents, you need to model patience and empathy. Try not to rush your kids or become irritable when they don't complete something right away. It's your job to teach them patience by waiting patiently in long lines, at the traffic light, or for your server on a crowded night at your favorite restaurant. Make sure they witness your giving others the benefit of the doubt as well. Defer the road rage comments during school drop-offs or when a minivan cuts you off. That person probably didn't do it on purpose. You are all just trying to get to school and work together.

- **Be optimistic.** Your personality definitely influences how your kids view the world. If we tend to be pessimistic, to be overly critical, or to have a bad attitude, our kids will engage the world in the same manner. Children naturally have positive demeanors. It's important as parents to give our children hope and teach them that anything is possible. Show your child how to set goals and how to work toward them. Share your dreams and allow your child to celebrate in your achievements. Being optimistic empowers your children to overcome life's challenges.

- **Be responsible.** Parents need to provide a safe, stable, and nurturing home environment. Do what you say you are going to do, and do what's right. Your children need to be able to depend on you and trust that you have their back. If you mess up, it's OK to apologize and try to correct your mistakes. Discuss what happened with your children, and ensure that everyone learns from the situation together. Move on and remember to be fair. That means allowing the same process for your kids when they make mistakes. It's unproductive and harmful to constantly bring up offenses from the past week or year when you get angry. After you've dealt with the problem, throw away the receipts. Teach, forgive, and *move on*!

Things can get intense when we are dealing with kids' behavior! As a parent, you're only human. There are times you're going to get frustrated and even angry.

You may yell and wish you had done things differently. But I promise, if you improve your parenting and selfie skills, you'll be able to manage your emotions and handle your kids' behavior and your home life appropriately. It starts with catching yourself in the moment before things "go bad." Take a deep breath, depart, collect yourself, and then respond to your child or the situation as the positive role model you are and want to be. Remember to check whether your expectations for your child are in line with their developmental capabilities. A mismatch between unrealistic parental expectations and developmentally appropriate (although unwanted) child behavior can be a setup for escalating frustrations that lead to abusive situations. Check yourself or check with your pediatrician to see whether you are expecting too much from your child at this time and for ways to manage the circumstances positively.

How Parents Maintain Model Status at All Times

1. Put yourself into time-out when you feel angry. Take ten and calm down. Just breathe.
2. Step away and talk your anger out with yourself. Yes, talk to yourself! This step helps you process and blow off steam. This is the time to be brutally honest, so you won't say anything hurtful to your child. I usually say, "Lord, help me before I. . . ." And sometimes I end up saying other things that make me laugh and then I feel better.
3. Develop a mantra or affirmations that you repeat to yourself when you are feeling tested. I often say, "Breathe, Candice"; "Step away, Candice"; or "Just ignore it, Candice."

Mom's Affirmation

I am Mom.
I am calm.
I am love.
I am patient.
I am kind.
I am the example.
I lead the way.
My kids will follow.

4. Get help from a friend or family member. My bestie Liz and I save each other's kids all the time. She's my voice of reason, and I'm her sounding board. My husband is the calm in all storms. He knows when I'm getting overwhelmed

and whisks the kids away when I need a breather. This helps me reset and get back to parenting in a peaceful and positive way. Don't feel bad if you're feeling emotionally tested. That's human! What matters is that you do or say the right thing and get the help you need to get back to modeling well.

5. If you can calmly express your feelings to your kids, do so. If not, keep breathing and counting until you have calmed down. Go for a walk, exercise, or write down your thoughts. Proceed once you are able to think clearly and communicate calmly.

6. Remember your puzzle pieces from Chapter 2, A Win-Win Approach: The High Five Essentials of Effective and Positive Parenting, and choose the right skill. Now that you're less emotional, plan how to address the problem.

Top Model Scenarios to Consider

Scenario 1

When your toddler writes on the sofa, give yourself a chance to calm down before you respond. You might realize that it wasn't what she did, but you had a rough day, and marker on the sofa was the last straw. You might also recall that this is typical toddler behavior, and maybe more supervision and better placement of the markers would be more helpful next time. So you should choose not to yell at her for writing on the sofa and instead show her that she should write on paper. Then have her help clean it up.

> **Scenario Skills:** Knowledge of Child Development and Parenting Skills (realistic expectations), Encouraging Positive Behavior (positive instructions), and Managing the Environment

Scenario 2

You realize it's 1:00 pm and your kids haven't had lunch or a nap, because you've been running around town to get last-minute items for their sister's birthday party at 5:00 pm. No wonder one child is throwing a tantrum and the other has been misbehaving for the past 30 minutes in Target. You take a break and feed and soothe them as best as you can. Your baby falls fast asleep, and your 8-year-old is full and ready to roll again. All is well.

> **Scenario Skills:** Discouraging and Correcting Negative Behavior (redirection and distraction) and Managing the Environment (being proactive, not reactive)

Scenario 3

You wake up to the sound of explosions and chatter. You realize it's your son, upstairs, playing video games loudly. The house rule is no screen time after bedtime. Sleep is important. As you get out of bed and go upstairs, you breathe and collect yourself, while saying to yourself, "No, he didn't wake me up at 3:00 am playing video games! I'm so sick of these darn games. . . ." The light bulb goes off in your head and you decide to collect the controllers, remotes, and phone at bedtime from now on. See if he gets around this one! Your son scrambles when he notices you at the top of the steps. He says, "Sorry, Mom. This was a Fortnite event I could only be part of now." As you unplug the game and take the controllers, you say, "What's the rule? I'll be keeping these until you show me you can follow the rules. Go to bed. Good night."

> **Scenario Skills:** Managing the Environment (setting limits and rules), Encouraging Positive Behavior (positive instructions), and Discouraging and Correcting Negative Behavior (logical consequences)

The steps to maintain model status can be used right away or several hours later. You may get stuck at step 2 for a whole day. That's OK. You don't have to react to anything or anyone right away. Sometimes, waiting will give you the time to formulate your best response. It's always best to calm down and think before you act and before you speak. You can say, "I'm too angry to discuss this right now," or "I don't want to do something I regret later," or "I don't know what to do, so we will address this tonight." Remember, doing nothing can be an effective disciplinary tool. And certainly, anticipating nothingness can give your child time to think about what they did wrong and how much it's going to cost them.

We should take the opportunity every day to lead by example. Model well, so your children will have the blueprint for impeccable behavior. Parents and other child caregivers are indeed top models!

Parenting Prescription

Model the behaviors you want your kids to display.

Chapter 5

Woosah . . . Mindfulness, Coping Skills, and Mindset

Calm down. Breathe. Chill out. Relax. *All words synonymous with "woosah," a word made popular in 2003 by the movie* Bad Boys II. *Over the years, woosah has become a mantra to remind us to get it together, "reel in" the rage, and take control of ourselves before we do something regretful. And that's what parents and other child caregivers need to do sometimes. WOOO-SAAAH!*

As I'm writing this chapter, the world is dealing with the devastating effects of the COVID-19 pandemic. Parents everywhere are struggling with having to manage everything at the same time: staying home with their kids, working, and worrying about keeping their family safe. Some have lost their means of income because of stay-at-home orders, worsening an already unstable financial situation. Suddenly, parents have a newfound respect for their children's teachers while trying to survive virtual learning from home. The kids are also struggling with being out of school, away from their friends, and expected to learn in a whole new way. For some students, school is a sacred place where they can eat and feel safe and nurtured. We also feel for the numerous graduates who are missing iconic milestones, like senior prom, graduation, and final sporting events. And our hearts go out to the many individuals whom we have tragically lost, or who are experiencing the illness, and their families who are affected. This virus affects us all in some way.

Never for one moment could we have imagined desolate streets, closed businesses, and people walking around grocery stores while wearing masks and gloves. In the beginning of the pandemic, it was hard to find toiletries such as toilet paper, hand sanitizer, and disinfectant wipes because of hoarding and extreme demand. In the United States, the "greatest country on earth," our health care system and frontline workers have struggled to maintain the equipment they need to protect

77

themselves, treat everyone, or test for the disease appropriately. Doctors, nurses, hospital staff, and other essential workers, our heroes, have died because they must report to work and can't stay home. Yet a small group of people storm the streets, without masks or regard for social distancing, to protest closures and stay-at-home orders. They are willing to risk it all under the guise of freedom for the ability to get back to life as usual despite a global public health crisis. We have experienced an uptick of fear, anxiety, depression, and violence as the trauma and stress of it all blanket the planet.

In Chapter 10, Be Aware: From ACEs to Healing, we'll talk about trauma and stress and how they can harm us and bring out the worst in us. Especially if we don't have the resilience and support we need to overcome that adversity. Depending on your child's age, they can experience stress in different ways, which can cause them to act out, so their behavior may change or worsen during these stressful times. In this chapter, I focus more on ways to cope, overcome, and heal. During uncertain times, including a pandemic, our children need us and look to us for safety, stability, and loving-kindness. We have to find positive ways to handle our problems, so they can still flourish and maintain their innocence. It's not their responsibility to help us get through this or any ordeal. Your children can't just automatically grow up and behave because you have too much on your plate. So don't rob them of their childhood. Let them be kids. It's your responsibility. You can do it!

Time out!

Remember, as you discipline during trying times, you are the teacher and children are your students. They are learning and they are also a work in progress. So don't take your frustrations out on them, even if they are partly the source. Give yourself and them a little grace.

The present moment is filled with joy and happiness. If you are attentive, you will see it.

—THICH NHAT HANH

Mindfulness

Practicing mindfulness is a gift. It's the gift of resilience or bouncing forward from adversity. It's calming, it's healing, and it strengthens your "selfie" skills, specifically self-awareness and self-control. It's an important piece in positive parenting.

Mindfulness is a healing practice through which you focus your mind in the heat of the moment, to be fully aware of your feelings, senses, and thoughts without interpretation or judgment. Think of it as an out-of-body experience. It involves being an active observer of your own emotions at that moment or during that experience. Practicing mindfulness affords insight, self-control, and appropriate actions or self-discipline. It includes breathing, guided imagery, and relaxation techniques to help reduce stress.

As we get bogged down in the challenges of daily living and responsibilities, our minds sometimes get stuck and full of negative thoughts and experiences. Mindfulness can facilitate gratitude and help us appreciate the beauty and the good that are all around us. Research shows that mindfulness strategies, such as meditation, can be effective against anxiety, depression, pain, insomnia, and even high blood pressure. They can also help improve attention span in children and reduce stress of professional burnout in adults.

Here is an example of a mindfulness exercise I have done often at home during the COVID-19 stay-at-home orders.

Example of a Mindfulness Exercise

As I step away from my family, I sit and just breathe—in slowly and out slowly.

I hear a garbage truck pull up outside. I think, "Good, someone's working. Be safe."

Breathe.

I hear the fire alarm beep. "Low battery," it says. I need to remind my husband, Derrick, to change that.

Breathe.

I hear my daughter playing with her doll, talking to it so kindly, sweetly telling it what to do.

Breathe.

I hear my son and husband discussing my son's schoolwork assignment. My son is frustrated and doesn't understand something, but my husband patiently explains it again.

Breathe.

(continued on next page)

I'm so glad my husband is home this week, away from the hospital, safe, and here to help me with our children.

Breathe.

I hear the rustle of the palm leaves in the wind and a bird chirping. I feel the sun on my face, beaming through the window. I see a clear blue sky, clouds sailing by, and vivid pink flowers in bloom.

Breathe.

So thankful for my breath. My family. My home. My life. My stomach growls. Oh, it's way past lunchtime. Duty calls . . .

Breathe.

That took about 3 minutes. I do it several times a day while I'm on a walk, during exercise, before bed when the house is quiet, or especially when I'm feeling agitated. I wish I remembered to do it more often. It keeps me refreshed, positive, thankful, patient, and calm. As my kids, work, and relationships chip away at my cool, it helps build my frustration tolerance and accept things as they currently are, live in the moment, and find joy.

There are so many ways to practice mindfulness. Some people use music, yoga, or incense as they look inward. Others start with mantras or affirmations before their deep breathing to stay positive and encourage themselves. Mindfulness can also work well with other therapies. There is no one or right way. Just start somewhere today and get your kids involved too. If you decide to introduce meditation to your kids, they can usually sit for as many minutes as their age. So for a 5-year-old, sitting for 5 minutes is an achievable goal. My kids and I do Yoga Pretzel cards, which demonstrate yoga moves and breathing techniques. My toddler loves this activity and usually initiates it. She throws the cards out onto the floor and picks a few different moves each time. I purposefully remind them to limit talking, speak softly, and breathe. See the "Did you know . . . ?" box on spiritual self-care in Chapter 3, Selfies, to explore other healing practices that you and your family could benefit from.

Mindful Parenting

Parenting mindfully is important in relieving some of the stress that parenting can sometimes create. How we interact with our children and significant others largely depends on our childhood experiences, learned behaviors, and how easily our stress responses are triggered. When our kids push our buttons, sometimes we don't think clearly or make rational decisions. We may behave selfishly and forget what our children need to have modeled in that moment.

Practicing mindful parenting helps us stop, think, and respond peacefully. When you manage your emotions this way, you teach your kids how to do the same when they are in conflict with others. Parents should be in the moment with their kids, whether good or bad. Focus your attention on what is happening and on your response. Acknowledge what you are feeling, and stay in the moment and breathe. Ten seconds can stop knee-jerk, emotionally driven reactions and help you respond in an instructive and nurturing way.

Another mindfulness technique that parents should know, because it works very well in the heat of the moment, is a **body scan.** It's like the previous mindfulness exercise, but this time, you focus on your body and how it feels to let thoughts come and go without judgment or response. Ideally, you focus on your toes. How do your feet feel? Then move slowly up your body and focus on your ankles, calves, and knees, and go all the way up to your head, noticing how each part feels at that moment. Be sure to breathe along the way. Again, this technique is a very soothing practice that will help you relax and can also help you get a good night's sleep. It works for kids as well.

Now consider the following common parent-child interactions:

- Do you ever feel embarrassed and frustrated when your toddler melts down in the middle of a restaurant or store? Do you feel everyone looking at you?
- How would you feel if you found out your teenager was experimenting with drugs? Would you feel disappointed, ashamed, or overwhelmed with stress?
- Do you ever feel angry when your child constantly talks back to you and does not listen or follow your instructions?

Let's examine these interactions mindfully. You will need to acknowledge your emotions. It's important to explore why you're really feeling this way and decide whether it's based in fear or reality. While doing this, try to understand how your child may be feeling, because their behaviors are definitely influenced by emotions as well. Remember, even though your child behaves negatively, they are not a "bad" person.

Scenario 1

Place yourself at the grocery store, trying to get everything on your list, when your child throws themselves onto the floor because you won't buy the candy they want. It feels as if the whole world is watching and shaking their head as they judge your every action. You feel embarrassed and ashamed and don't know what to do. You worry that others may think you are stupid or inadequate as a parent, because you should be able to control your child's behavior better. Parent shaming is based in fear, not reality.

Parent Shaming

Don't parent shame yourself, and don't let anyone parent shame you either.

You need to understand that the whole world isn't watching you in those moments and every parent can relate to that situation or has been there before. You are not alone.

The truth is, all children misbehave. It's perfectly normal for a child to make a poor choice or have a bad day, tantrums included. Parents experience this as well, don't we? If you have a child with ongoing problem behaviors, no one knows your situation and how hard things can be at times. The people who may be judging you usually don't have kids anyway.

Please don't act on your perceptions or mistreat your child to please onlookers. Put your blinders on: be in the moment with your child and ignore everyone else. Don't worry about what others think—for example, the well-meaning grandma, the unsolicited advice giver at church, or the disapproving shopper in aisle 6. Be confident in your parenting skills, be consistent, and focus on what's best for your family.

Again, take ten. *Breathe.* Woosah before you say or do anything. This allows your "thinking brain" (prefrontal cortex) to overcome your "primitive brain" (amygdala) that just wants to snap. Now you are in control of yourself and not worrying about controlling someone else. Sometimes during this step, we realize that it was just our overthinking things and nothing needed to be said or done. We should just let the experience pass and move on. Talk the conflict out and resolve it peacefully. Share your perspective, and listen to your child's point of view without interruption or judgment.

Scenario 2

Think about how you would feel if you found drug paraphernalia in your teenage son's bedroom. It's totally reasonable to be overcome with fear, anger, and disappointment and to want to immediately fly off the handle and lock your son in his room forever to prevent him from using drugs again. This is a parent's worst fear. So take a moment to settle down. Resist the urge to respond to your teen in anger. Call a trusted friend or family member, or reach out to a professional, for help. Plan out your response.

By all means, be honest and tell your son how angry and disappointed you are with his poor choice. But focus on why your teen tried drugs and ways to prevent further use. Now is the time to plan and prepare for a safer future. Connect with your teen, listen, and try to understand. Reiterate the dangers of drugs and alcohol, and set your expectation that he will refrain from using them. And a consequence may include more supervision, limited privacy, or even drug testing until you trust that he is drug-free.

Scenario 3

When your middle schooler constantly talks back, refuses to listen, or fails to follow instructions, this misbehavior can be extremely frustrating. It is a top-tier concern for parents that can create harmful parent-child interactions if handled incorrectly. Parents should recognize when they are feeling triggered and take the appropriate steps to calm themselves. I recommend using a safe word that signals both of you to discontinue the conversation, retreat to your corners, and calm down. You can always revisit the situation later, when you are better able to address it positively. If this is a frequent problem with you and your child, please get professional help to figure out the nature of your turmoil and a pathway to a healthy relationship with your child. You should be able to talk about anything peacefully.

Another pet peeve of many parents is when their kids whine, nag, or complain all the time. I, too, have experienced this. One beautiful afternoon, my husband and I decided to take a bike ride with the kids on a day that was cooler than normal, here in Florida. Well, it was the weekend and prime time for my son to play video games with his friends. He didn't want to go. He pleaded, grunted, and came up with all kinds of reasons why we shouldn't ride out. We ignored his efforts and stood our ground on getting out of the house for fresh air and exercise. He kept up this behavior until we reached our halfway point and I had had enough. My efforts to ignore this behavior had failed. I heard Darth Vader's famous words, "The Force is strong with this one," and tried to remain calm.

I took a deep breath and got his attention. I asked, "Can you be in the moment with us? Can you try to enjoy the bike ride, soak up the sun, and feel this amazing breeze? One day, you will be all grown-up and unable to ride bikes with Mommy, Daddy, and your little sister. And then you'll say, 'I wish I could ride bikes with my family like we used to.' Can you do this for me, please?" It worked like magic! His attitude changed. He agreed and seemed to enjoy the rest of the ride (or at least acted as if he did). And so did we.

If I hadn't calmed myself first and used my mindfulness skills, I might have yelled, threatened, or punished my son harshly. But it didn't take all of that effort to reach him and manage the situation positively and to show him how to handle conflict appropriately in the future.

Coping Skills

The COVID-19 pandemic has certainly taught all of us new and innovative ways to cope with the stressors of life. Students are learning on their computers at home and in ways never imagined. We have been distanced from our families and friends but stay connected through FaceTime, Skype, and Zoom meetings. Netflix, celebrity Instagram parties, and neighborhood efforts, like stuffed animal safaris, have kept us all entertained. Also, we now know that most of our jobs can be done from home. Another silver lining is Mother Nature seems very happy! Early in the pandemic during quarantine, pictures of animals roaming the streets, major cities being free of smog, and clear, snow-capped mountain peaks went viral in the media. And the one thing we've learned is that we are all in this together.

Unfortunately, in individual homes and communities, there may be challenges that add even more pressure, like domestic violence, mental health crises, health problems, and poverty, just to name a few. With all that parents have to juggle, it makes sense that they sometimes fall short of being the best versions of themselves. However, practicing mindfulness and having a set of positive coping skills that work for you are key to making the best of a trying situation for yourself and your family.

To cope is to deal with problems. Coping skills are the things we do, think, or feel that help us deal with those problems. Coping skills can be positive, effective, and healthy. Or they can be negative, ineffective, and unhealthy.

Positive Coping Skills

When life gives us lemons, we can use positive coping skills to help us make lemonade. Keep a few of the strategies from the following chart in your back pocket to use the next time lemons come your way:

Type of coping	Strategies
Problem-focused	Ask for help, make a to-do list, organize, create healthy boundaries, discuss the issue
Emotion-focused	Exercise, take a bath, meditate or pray, give yourself a pep talk, practice gratitude, enjoy humor
Proactive	Plan, recite a mantra or an affirmation, rely on a supportive ecosystem, adjust your expectations/attitude

Negative Coping Skills

When you try to deal with a problem in a way that causes more harm than good, you are using negative coping skills. Do yourself a favor and try to rid your life of negative coping skills. They may feel right or good at the time, but they aren't good for you or the situation. Using them can create problems and patterns of behaviors that are counterproductive to being your best in life and in parenting.

Oftentimes people don't realize that their responses represent negative coping. If the problem or pattern keeps resurfacing or worsens, you're most likely handling it in the wrong way.

Avoid the following behaviors when feeling overwhelmed:

- Medicating and numbing problems with drugs, alcohol, or other risky behaviors
- Avoidance, isolation, or suppressing feelings
- Blame
- Overindulgence with overeating, oversleeping, or overspending
- Denial
- Complaining excessively

Growth Mindset

In the book *Mindset: The New Psychology of Success,* Stanford psychologist Carol Dweck explores how our beliefs influence success. She discusses both fixed and growth mindsets and how adjusting what we believe can make all the difference in every area of our lives—parenting, business, and relationships. A person with a fixed mindset believes that personality, intelligence, and other creative abilities are set and there is little the individual can do to change. This is a setup for striving for success and avoiding failure in an effort to appear smart or prove yourself to others. The fixed mindset person tends to avoid challenges, give up easily, ignore constructive criticism, and feel threatened by others' success, which negatively affects reaching one's full potential.

A person with a growth mindset, on the other hand, believes that personality and abilities can be nurtured and developed. They are usually lifelong learners who welcome challenges, push through failures, maximize effort, learn from criticism, and find inspiration in the success of others. Therefore, they are highly successful in their endeavors. In her book, Dweck states, "The view you adopt for yourself profoundly affects the way you lead your life. It can determine whether you become the person you want to be." How can we use a growth mindset to be successful parents and positive disciplinarians? We can

- Reject the notion that we are who we are and can't change.
- Unlearn and learn to improve our parenting skills to benefit our daily interactions with our children.
- Strive to be the best versions of ourselves as parents, professionals, and significant others.
- Reprogram our thinking, regroup from our failures, and make a fresh start at any time.

- Foster a growth mindset in our children at an early age by praising all of their efforts, whether they're successful or not.
- Never give up on our kids and always try to help them learn and grow.

That said, some parents are under incredible amounts of stress related to societal influences that are out of their control, such as poverty, crime, and discrimination that affect their ability to manage parental stress. Never give up. Lean on your faith, gather strength and support from "your village," and ask for help. You are not alone, and there are people waiting to assist you during these difficult times.

This part of the book has focused on the adults. Parents must own how they contribute to dynamics with their children. Although there will always be stressors involved with parenting and caring for children, you should learn ways to work on yourself, manage your emotions, and use effective strategies that will empower everyone to make positive choices.

In my opinion, the best parents are those who self-reflect, foster self-care, model positive behaviors, and maintain a positive mindset in parenting. These parents will successfully raise happy, healthy, well-behaved children. Where are you on this parenting journey? Are you where you want to be? In what areas do you need to improve? Start there!

Parenting Prescription

Keep a positive mindset and use positive coping skills to ease the stress of life and parenting. And don't forget to woosah!

PART 4

Child Basics

Act Like a Parent but Think Like a Child

Children are human beings to whom respect is due, superior to us by reason of their innocence and of the greater possibilities of their future.

—Maria Montessori

As a pediatrician, I have a job that goes beyond performing well-child visits and caring for my patients when they are sick and feeling unwell. One of my most important jobs as a doctor is probably prevention. Pediatricians help parents prevent and identify all sorts of problems by monitoring their child's growth and developmental milestones, recommending healthy habits, and helping them anticipate and prepare for the phases and stages to come. For example, during the 6-month well-child visit, I remind parents that their baby will start crawling around everywhere and being more mobile in the next few months. I advise that it's time for baby gates, electrical outlet covers, and other injury prevention items. All of these reminders help prevent injury to the child.

You always want to be that proactive parent and make your home safe by childproofing it before your child reaches their accident-prone stage. Emergency departments care for thousands of children who are injured from falls down steps, burns from hot stoves or hot liquids, unintentional ingestions of chemicals and medications, and drownings. These tragedies are all preventable with adequate adult supervision and childproofing of the environment.

Just as I can predict the next developmental milestones with my knowledge of child development and help parents keep their kids safe, I can anticipate child behaviors and help parents discipline their kids appropriately. And parents . . . so can you! This book has already highlighted one of the essential pieces of positive parenting, Knowledge of Child Development and Parenting Skills, to maintain realistic expectations and effectively guide and teach your children. There are critical needs during child development that must be met for children to grow and thrive appropriately. We discuss those stages and offer ways to optimize them. We also make sense of typical behaviors and misbehaviors at each developmental stage and strategize to encourage behaviors we want to happen and manage behaviors we don't want to happen. The ultimate goal is to empower our kids to do all of this troubleshooting for themselves successfully one day.

In the following chapters, we get age specific. Please note, behaviors begin in the period they are mentioned but may continue for some time. So you can use the same management skills even as your child gets older, if the behavior persists. Remember, we're slowly combining all the positive parenting puzzle pieces to create a peaceful home life and happy, healthy, well-behaved kids. Information from prior chapters is foundational and always at play when we are considering these last few chapters.

Chapter 6

Early Childhood, or the Critical Years: Birth to 3 Years

The infant and toddler years are critical because they are fundamental in shaping the adult years. This is the period of most rapid brain development, with more than a million neuronal connections forming per second, also making it a highly sensitive and vulnerable period. Years 0 to 3 set the foundation for future learning, behavior, and health, which makes them susceptible to interactions among the child's genes, environment, and experiences.

Therefore, parent-child interactions greatly influence growth and development. Babies aren't on autopilot. They need a lot of support to have a healthy start early in life. With parental support, miraculously newborns go from only sucking, pooping, and crying after birth to walking, talking, and feeding themselves around the age of 1 year. Babies who miss adequate support have been shown to be at increased risk of developing speech delay, learning, and behavior and emotional problems.

INFANCY: BIRTH TO 1 YEAR

What Can My Baby Do?

Use the following charts to gauge your baby's development. Are they where they should be? Are your expectations appropriate? Some babies may have health conditions that keep them from reaching typical developmental milestones. Talk with your pediatrician to assess what your baby can do. Call your pediatrician if you ever have any concerns that your baby is not meeting these milestones.

What My Baby Can Do: Birth to 3 Months

☐ I communicate my needs through crying or fussiness.

☐ I am discovering my body and how it works.

☐ I am learning from you and others in my environment. I turn toward sound and follow people and objects with my eyes.

☐ My sight is still developing. Get close so I can see you and interact with you. I may start smiling and make cute noises.

What My Baby Can Do: 3 to 6 Months

☐ I am learning how to move my body. I reach and grab things, roll, sit up with help, and get into a crawling position.

☐ I can communicate better through babbling, responding, and facial expressions.

☐ I am getting used to routines—time to sleep, nap, or eat.

☐ I am paying more attention to what's going on in my environment. I like to look in the mirror and recognize familiar faces.

What My Baby Can Do: 6 to 9 Months

☐ I am an explorer. I test things out to discover what happens. But I have no concept of safety.

☐ I am sitting up on my own, crawling, and working on standing. I can switch objects from one hand to the other.

☐ I may be afraid of strangers.

☐ I am putting babbling sounds together, like "hihi," "baba," "gugu," "dada," and "kaka," and repeating sounds.

☐ I love to laugh.

What My Baby Can Do: 9 Months to 1 Year

☐ I mimic what I see and hear.

☐ I can say my first words and understand some things I hear, such as "No."

☐ I use a pincerlike grasp to pick up small items. I can pull off my socks, I can clap my hands, and I can stand or may be walking.

☐ I'm starting to remember where things are and how they work.

☐ I may have stranger anxiety.

What Does My Baby Need From Me?

There are very important needs infants have that make a difference in how well they develop. Obviously, they need the basics of life as all children do—for example, proper nutrition, safe housing, and access to health care, which depend on parental or caregiver resources. Then there are intangibles that are just as impactful, such as developing a secure attachment bond, nurturing, and responding.

Secure Attachment Bond

The attachment bond is the emotional connection between you and your baby that is built on your nonverbal communication interactions. A parent and baby bond and attach when they connect emotionally, building the baby's trust and sense of safety and calm with the parent. Interactions such as gazing into each other's eyes, cuddling, and baby talk help form a secure attachment bond. Healthy relationship qualities like empathy, love, and the ability to interact well with others are all first learned in early infancy during the attachment bond. Establishing a secure attachment bond influences the way your infant's brain organizes and how your child will develop behaviorally, emotionally, intellectually, and physically.

In a study of 14,000 US infants, 40% lacked secure attachment to their parents, which put them at risk for delayed speech, learning problems, and behavioral and emotional problems for a lifetime. For example, postpartum blues and postpartum depression make it difficult for mothers to securely attach with their babies and can endanger both lives. Recognizing these conditions and getting help for them is the best thing a mother can do for herself and her child. Talk with your obstetrician or your baby's pediatrician if you are struggling to bond and attach with your child.

Nurturing

Nurturing a baby goes beyond just caring for physical needs like feeding them and bathing them. It also includes the things parents do to support their baby's growth and development. Babies need attention, affection, and to feel loved. They need to experience play and tummy time. They enjoy when you sing and read to them. Every kiss, cuddle, and comforting sway communicates your love for your child and helps nurture their growth and development.

Responding

When your baby tries to communicate with you by cooing, smiling, grimacing or crying, or reaching out to your face, it's important to respond positively by talking to, smiling at, gazing at, or consoling your child. These "serve and return" interactions help build your child's brain and optimize their growth and development. And just as you will use cues to tell your children what you need from them, your baby will use cues to tell you what they need from you. You'll soon learn your baby's hungry cry, dirty diaper look, and "I want to play" sounds. Observe your baby and respond to them appropriately. Singing, talking, reading, and smiling with your infant also strengthen your connection with them.

It's a myth that always responding to your baby's every need spoils them. Responding, nurturing, and bonding with your baby all build trust and a sense of safety. These strengthen the parent-child relationship and make it more likely that your child will learn to self-soothe, regulate emotions, listen to you, follow your instructions, and become more independent as they grow. So in my opinion, you can't spoil your baby enough.

However, please don't do anything unsafe to make your baby happy. No matter how much your baby cries in their crib, *do not* put them into the bed with you to help them sleep. This is unsafe. You should check on them when they cry or should feed, rock, and swaddle them to safely soothe them back to sleep. A baby's cry can be very stressful, so if you feel overwhelmed, ask for help or step away for a few minutes to calm yourself. In these moments, remember: safety first!

Early Learning and Play

Believe it or not, infants are curious observers of their environment. Infants can do more and more each day in the areas of thinking, problem-solving, and learning new things. This period is the perfect time to set the foundation for early learning. By reading to your baby, singing nursery rhymes, and playing with them with age-appropriate toys, you are constantly teaching them. Putting in quality time and keeping your baby engaged are also key to positive behavior. Try to introduce baby sign language, which can help your child communicate their needs even though they don't have the words yet. This may cut down on some of their emotional outbursts, simply because they're better at telling you what they want.

Here is a list of early learning activities and what skills they're building.

Motor skills	Social-emotional skills	Cognitive skills	Communication skills
Tummy/floor time (childproofed, for safety)	Tell your baby what you are doing.	Read books.	Talk to your baby, make eye contact, or imitate sounds.
Old-fashioned toys—for example, blocks, rattles	Making faces, having your baby look in the mirror	Sing songs—"This Little Piggy," "Row Row Row Your Boat," or "Wheels on the Bus."	Sign language

Motor skills	Social-emotional skills	Cognitive skills	Communication skills
Play center bouncer	Daily routines— meals, naps, bedtime (reading *Goodnight Moon,* playing lullabies)	Play games like peekaboo, pat-a-cake, or "Where is it?"/ "Here it is!"	"Hi" and "Bye"
Play with textures such as water, putty, or paint	Playful tickle Name emotions— "I'm happy," "I'm sad."	Counting, colors, ABCs	Naming objects, how they feel, what they do, or what sounds they make
Pots and pans	Sharing—"My turn"/"Your turn"	Building blocks	Say *mama, dada, baba, eat,* or other short words.

Why Does My Baby Do That, and What Can I Do About It?

Crying

All babies cry, so expect crying and accept it. Crying is the younger infant's only means of communication. They cry to communicate hunger, a soiled diaper, sleepiness, or just wanting to be held. Some babies have colic, which occurs sometime from 3 weeks to 3 months of age and is defined as frequent, prolonged, severe crying or fussiness in an infant who is otherwise healthy. We don't know the cause of colic, but the good news is that it will resolve, usually by 3 months of age.

Other little babies can have a feisty temperament. Temperament is an individual emotional and behavioral style. Unfortunately, babies can be treated differently according to their temperament. For instance, I had twin patients who behaved very differently as infants. Their mom labeled one twin as easy, so sweet, and her big boy, whereas the other twin was seen as mean, always crying, and fussy, and she wondered what was wrong with him. I explained that they were both healthy and just had different temperaments. I discouraged negative labels and encouraged her to accept, engage, and parent her babies as individuals and not to make comparisons.

Regardless of the cause, when a baby's crying is excessive, some parents may find it tough to handle. It's just a stage, so please hold on. It will get better. Remember in these stressful situations to never shake or hit a baby! If you feel yourself getting frustrated, put your baby into a safe place and walk away until you calm down. Having a plan to calm your nerves, get some sleep, and settle your baby will help you through this stage. Here are a few tips.

- Divide and conquer with your significant other or a trusted family member to lessen the stress.
- Sleep when your baby sleeps.
- Alter the environment to promote a normal sleep-wake cycle. Keep the surroundings bright and active during the day and quiet and dark at night.
- Take short breaks away from your baby, even if you have to leave them safe in the crib.
- Maintain appropriate hygiene, nutrition, and exercise.
- Use safe soothing techniques (ie, a bouncer, a swing, a car ride, hold your baby and move around, swaddle them, feed them, check their diaper, give them a bath, check them for illness).
- Call or visit your pediatrician if you're concerned that something may be wrong with your baby.

Tantrums

In late infancy, 9 to 12 months of age, your baby's crying may evolve into "falling out," or throwing things down to the ground when they are upset. This is usually when I see parents start to use negative disciplinary tactics, such as spanking or yelling. This is very frustrating for parents, because they see it as a sign of disrespect or a predictor of negative behavior in the future when, in all honesty, most, if not all, children behave this way at one time or another. Falling out morphs into meltdowns or tantrums, which are iconic in the toddler period to come. Again, it's important for parents to understand that this is a very common stage that all babies go through. Getting through it requires you to do exactly what you want your child to do—to calm down. When you have good emotional intelligence, model self-control, and teach children social-emotional skills, they will learn to regulate themselves emotionally sooner rather than later.

For the infant who "falls out," this is the perfect misbehavior that parents can try to redirect or distract by being silly or offering a toy. However, don't give in to the misbehavior. For example, if your baby is eating cereal off the floor and falls out when you remove it from their hand, don't give them the cereal; instead, offer them something they can play with on the floor. If redirection or distraction doesn't work, remove your attention. Model deep breathing, and at the first sign of the child's calming down, console and acknowledge the child and move on.

Hitting, Biting, and Other Acts of Aggression

As mentioned earlier, infants struggle to control themselves emotionally, because they don't have the best communication skills at this age. They have not learned the vocabulary to express themselves. Imagine if you couldn't express yourself or argue your case. You might become angry and lash out too. As babies develop speech and language skills, they learn to use their words to express emotions instead of their hands and tantrums to talk for them. It takes time, but with your support, they should get there by the preschool years. So hold on!

Not all hitting and biting are aggressive or mean-spirited. Sometimes, babies are just doing what has been modeled, being playful, or even testing out the texture of your arm.

When your baby hits or bites, be consistent and clearly tell them what to do (ie, "Nice hands," "Hands to yourself," or "We don't bite"). You can also ignore mild aggressions that aren't harmful or unkind. When kids get this behavior right, be sure to praise them. And don't forget to check the behaviors you show your children, because they will repeat them. So biting your child or hitting them back is an inappropriate response.

The focus on early discipline should be to prepare the infant for later understanding, but parents should not expect verbal commands, correction, or reasoning to manage infant behavior. Remember, appropriate disciplinary skills that you may find useful during infancy are

- Withholding your attention
- Telling or showing your child what to do (6–12 months)
- Redirection and distraction
- Positive reinforcement

Toddlerhood: 1 to 3 Years

What Can My Toddler Do?

Use the following charts to gauge your toddler's development. Are they where they should be? Are your expectations appropriate?

What My Toddler Can Do: 12 to 18 Months

- ☐ I am walking, saying more words, scribbling, and feeding myself.
- ☐ I play alongside other kids, but I struggle with sharing because I think everything is mine.
- ☐ I love pretend play and imitating others.
- ☐ When I get upset, I may throw a tantrum.
- ☐ I point to things I want and say, "No," or "Stop."
- ☐ I point to show things that are interesting to me.

What My Toddler Can Do: 18 to 24 Months

- ☐ I can run, jump, climb, build a block tower, and try to get dressed.
- ☐ I have a vocabulary of 30 to 50 words and speak in 2-word sentences.

(continued on next page)

☐ I have many emotions and at times refuse to adhere to instructions.

☐ I can follow 2-step familiar commands with a gesture (eg, "Bring me your socks and shoes," "Sit down and eat").

What My Toddler Can Do: 24 to 30 Months

☐ I want to do things by myself.

☐ I am starting to play with others and like being with other kids.

☐ I'm interested in going to the potty.

☐ My sentences contain 2 to 4 words.

☐ I can follow a 2-step familiar command without a gesture.

What My Toddler Can Do: 30 to 36 Months

☐ I'll test limits, test boundaries, and show defiance.

☐ I'm able to communicate what I want and express emotions (eg, use my words).

☐ I can play in a small group.

☐ I can follow a 2-step new command without a gesture.

☐ By 36 months, I can draw a circle, sort shapes and colors, kick a ball, and run fairly well.

What Does My Toddler Need From Me?

Patience and Understanding

Toddlerhood is made up of 5 distinct stages. As shown in the charts, a 12- to 18-month-old toddler is quite different from a toddler who is 30 to 36 months old. The 3-year-old is more capable in the areas of physical development, speech, emotional control, and cognitive reasoning. As children advance through the stages of life, caregivers should understand these milestones and adjust their expectations and disciplinary practices to match the level of the child.

That said, the poster child for toddlerhood is a kid who has lots of energy, gets into everything, goes from happy to mad quickly, makes big messes, wants to do it all themselves, believes everything belongs to them, and doesn't seem to listen or do anything you ask. These are fun and challenging times. It will take all the patience and understanding you can muster to navigate this period successfully. Your child really needs this from you, because it's who they are for the moment.

Independence

Toddlers hunger for being independent. They want to do what they want, when they want, and how they want. But obviously, they don't know what's best, so it's up to parents to intervene on their behalf. This often leads to a "Clash of the Titans." You, the authority figure, versus a strong-willed child. In these moments, try to take your child's behavior for what it is—a struggle for independence and free will. So don't take it personally when they get upset after you take over toothbrushing or pick their outfit. Support their development of self-care skills by modeling, allowing them to try things on their own, and giving them choices. They will become capable and confident, and you'll have less power struggles.

Early Detection and Early Intervention

It's critical that all children receive regular well-child visits for many reasons. One of the most important reasons for these is to help monitor that a child is developing properly and meeting their milestones. Some children display concerning behaviors due to delays in development or to developmental-related conditions such as speech delay. Recognizing these concerns early and addressing them quickly can make all the difference in a child's future. A child who can't hear well will have difficulty following your commands. A toddler who struggles with speech may communicate emotionally with tantrums and aggression like an infant. Sometimes a pediatrician will notice more extreme behaviors that may raise concerns for neurodevelopmental conditions, such as autism spectrum disorder.

What Parents Should Know About the Early Signs of Autism Spectrum Disorder

During your baby's well-child visit screenings at 18 months old and 24 months old, your pediatrician will look for behaviors that may raise concerns for neurodevelopmental conditions. If you notice any of the following issues in your child, talk with your pediatrician about your concerns. Here are examples of how a child with autism spectrum disorder might act.

► Has poor eye contact
► Doesn't respond to their parents' smile or facial expressions
► Doesn't look at what their parents are pointing to
► Doesn't point at objects or try to get others to look at an object
► Doesn't initiate play with their parents, such as peekaboo or pat-a-cake
► Doesn't bring or show things to their parents

(continued on next page)

- ▶ Lacks appropriate facial expressions
- ▶ Can't read facial expressions
- ▶ Doesn't show concern for others
- ▶ Has difficulty making friends or is uninterested in doing so
- ▶ Has speech delay
- ▶ Shows repetitive behaviors like rocking or flapping their hands
- ▶ Has difficulty with change
- ▶ Is obsessed with certain activities or objects
- ▶ Doesn't seem to feel pain
- ▶ May have sensitivities to sounds, textures, lights, and smells

Why Does My Toddler Do That, and What Can I Do About It?

As mentioned earlier, toddlers are a handful. Their behaviors are hyperactive, emotionally unstable, oppositional, and totally awesome all at the same time. When your child turns 18 months of age, you will notice the emergence of their consciousness: defiance, tantrums, and the terrible twos will all begin. That's why toddlerhood is called the "terrible twos"! Well, I call it the "terrible 18 months to threenager period," which I'm trying to survive as I write this book. So what's really going on during toddlerhood?

I, Me, and Mine Stage

Toddlers can sometimes seem selfish, seem demanding, or think the world revolves around them. They are in an egocentric stage of development, according to psychologist Jean Piaget, which explains why you may be hearing "I, me, and mine" all the time. Therefore, toddlers struggle to view a situation from another person's point of view or show empathy toward another person's feelings.

But with everything, toddlers are learning. Around 18 months, children start to understand the likes and dislikes of others. By 24 months, they can tell the emotional state of another person. And by 36 months, they are starting to recognize the likes, dislikes, and emotions of others. They have not mastered empathy but show developing empathy skills: they try to help (eg, pick something up that a parent drops), they try to comfort a sad friend, and they show concern if a baby is crying. Balancing their ego and early empathy is tough for a toddler. So expecting a 2- or 3-year-old to know how to share is unfair. By all means, parents need to teach and model sharing, but their child will not master it until the preschool to early school-age years.

Toddlers are also always on the move because they're curious about the world around them. They're superactive observers and explorers of their environment. This process is how they learn, develop, and gain new skills. That's why, as a parent, understanding your kid's developmental stages is important, so you know what skills they have mastered and should be learning next.

Emotional Roller Coaster

We've discussed how time-outs, or time-to-calm-down periods, can be useful in managing tantrums at this age. In late toddlerhood, it's important to start giving kids the words to describe their feelings and to self-soothe, because they still struggle with regulating their emotions. Acknowledging their emotions makes them feel loved and supported and lays an early foundation for developing empathy.

Consider the following scenarios:

Child's reaction	Parent's response
Child has a meltdown literally over spilled milk.	"Uh oh, you spilled your milk? It's OK. It was an accident. I know you're sad, but you can get some more."
Child throws his shoe across the room because he can't get it on in the right way.	"Is that a good choice?" Then, follow up with, "I know you're mad, because you can't get your shoe on, but we don't throw things. You can ask for help and I will help you. OK?"
Child hits when she can't have her way.	"It's OK to be upset but it's not OK to hit. Keep your hands to yourself, please."

Here are other ways to minimize emotional outbursts in toddlers.

- Keep a routine so your child knows what to expect.
- Give kids plenty of attention, and engage them with age-appropriate play.
- Limit screen time. It almost always ends in disaster.
- Supervise children, but allow them plenty of space to explore, be creative, and make a mess.

Nonadherence

I believe that most disobedience in toddlerhood is not intentional or mean-spirited; rather, it is age-appropriate testing and a part of typical development. Toddlers don't have the best self-control, judgment, and reasoning skills at this age. They are by nature doers and not thinkers. They catch more of what they see and hear rather than what you teach them. When they say no or ignore you or refuse to do what you are asking, remember that they are driven to do things in their way. So to navigate these struggles, play to your child's need for being independent by giving them choices, allowing them to make decisions, and only intervening for safety or when they ask for assistance. Patience is required during this phase.

Establishing structure and routines and setting limits help control your toddler's environment. Positive and negative reinforcement, countdown cues, and various consequences can also help manage the behavior of toddlers who don't want to follow instructions. And always fall back on your loving and secure relationship with your child to melt their resistance. I've witnessed my daughter give in to a soft "But I want you to" from our nanny, Ms Dana. Then my daughter reluctantly says, "Okayyy." Finesse, not force, is key.

Parenting Prescription

The critical years, birth to 3 years, form a foundation that lasts for a lifetime. Build a strong foundation!

Chapter 7

Preschool Period: 3 to 5 Years

What Can My Preschooler Do?

Use the following chart to gauge your preschooler's development. Are they where they should be? Are your expectations appropriate?

What My Preschooler Can Do: 3 to 5 Years

- ☐ I can ride a tricycle, hop and then skip, take the stairs, use scissors, draw basic shapes and letters, and dress and undress myself.
- ☐ I know the difference between girls and boys and recognize physical differences.
- ☐ I speak clearly.
- ☐ I cooperate with other kids and can negotiate conflict.
- ☐ I can retell a story or sing a song.
- ☐ I am very imaginative and struggle with separating fantasy from reality.

What Does My Preschooler Need From Me?

Preschool children still need your patience and understanding, because although things are getting better, they have yet to master some toddler challenges. They're still behaving egocentrically, seeking independence, and thinking concretely. The good news is that they're growing, learning, and maturing more and more each day. Speech becomes nearly clear, easing communication and emotions. Your preschooler is probably more talkative, imaginative, and curious, which is why this stage is often called "The Wonder Years."

Answers to Questions

All you may be hearing these days is "Why?" "Why?" and "Why?" or some other question.

> *"Eat your food." "But why? I don't like it."*
> *"Time for bed." "Why, Mommy? I'm not sleepy."*
> *"Why is it taking so long?" "Why did he do that?"*
> *"Why is it raining?" "Why is the water cold?" "What are they doing over there?"*

Although the ever-present "Why?" can be annoying and time consuming, preschoolers aren't trying to get on your nerves. They're not only seeking answers to the thoughts popping up in their heads but also trying to be noticed so they can talk with you—the one person they trust for answers. So set aside quality time to talk with your child, listen, and answer their silly questions. Call it "Ask me anything" time. Set a timer for 10 to 15 minutes. When the time is up, reassure your child that they'll be able to do it again another time, but now you need to do something else. You can also ask for a talking break and give your child something else to do instead. Don't just ignore their questions.

Also, instead of answering your child's questions, reply with the same or a similar question that will help them answer the question themselves. For example, if they ask, "Why is the water cold?" you can say, "Why do you think the water is cold?" Your child will come up with answers, so be sure to praise them and say, "Good answer!" (with claps). This encourages them to become thinkers and to figure things out for themselves. It also sends the message that you value their thoughts and believe in them.

Life Skills

Teach your child how to be a good and kind human by instilling peace, inclusion, and empathy toward others. Allow them to have playdates to help build their social skills. Try to arrange a playdate with someone your child knows or has met at preschool. These are wonderful opportunities for your child to exercise, practice sharing and taking turns, and engage in play with others kids. When conflicts arise, turn them into teachable moments to promote conflict resolution skills. Continue to help your child gain self-control and emotional regulation by learning to recognize and master emotional interactions. Remember, parents are kids' first teachers, and kids first learn how to navigate this thing called life from you.

Teach your child by modeling the ability to manage your emotions in a positive way. Every emotion—happiness, sadness, anger, fear, shame, guilt, and jealousy, to name a few—should be validated. Never dismiss your child's feelings. Help them process emotions, and help them come up with an appropriate response. Teach kids responsibility. Give them small chores around the house to let them know they're needed and the family depends on them. They can put their shoes where those belong, hang up their coat, and clean up their toys. Again, praise and reward them for being good helpers.

Encourage your child to be a "big boy" or "big girl" or "big kid," and praise their self-help skills. Allow them to brush their teeth or to pick out an outfit and get dressed alongside you as much as you can. Be patient when they put their shirt on backward or their pants on inside out. What is important is that you let them try to do it themselves. Let them be your little chef in the kitchen and help with simple tasks like stirring ingredients, pouring them, or even cracking eggs. Believe it or not, all of this helps create a happy, healthy, well-behaved child.

School Readiness

It's important to ensure that your child is ready to enter kindergarten. Children who aren't ready can struggle behaviorally and academically in the classroom. Not to mention, it can have a negative impact on their self-confidence and self-esteem. We've already discussed early learning in toddlerhood, but now it's time to really focus on learning—your preschooler is more than capable. Before your children start kindergarten, make sure they have the following school skills packed in their backpacks:

Get Ready for School Skills

- ► Listen and follow 3-step commands.
- ► Be kind and show empathy.
- ► Communicate needs.
- ► Dress, feed, and clean up after yourself.
- ► Share, take turns, and work in group activities.
- ► Sing a song or retell a story.
- ► Match and sort objects.
- ► Know basic shapes and colors.
- ► Know numbers and count.
- ► Know the alphabet, and recognize some letters and sounds.
- ► Know some sight words.
- ► Write your name.

The best way to help your child achieve these is to make learning fun. Put down your phone or laptop, and carve out short periods each day for playful learning with your child. Limit screen time, and if you're concerned about your child's ability to learn or retain information, talk with your pediatrician and consider an evaluation.

Before 3 years of age, your child can receive developmental services through early intervention programs. At 3 years of age, your public school can evaluate your child for possible special education needs, such as speech therapy, in all 50 states according to the the Individuals with Disabilities Education Act. Your pediatrician can also asses your child by using various screening tools and/or can refer your child to a developmental pediatrician or private speech, physical, or occupational therapist. Early detection and early intervention of developmental delays are crucial in preventing more complex and potentially lifelong disorders and disabilities. A "wait and see" approach often becomes a "wait to fail" decision that parents regret.

Why Does My Preschooler Do That, and What Can I Do About It?

The preschool period is very similar to the toddler period, but things are improving. The behaviors of preschoolers are more manageable as they learn and mature. Emotional outbursts become shorter and less frequent, because they're learning to use their words to express their feelings and figuring things out for themselves. Judgment and impulsivity are improving. Preschoolers are learning what's right and what's wrong and better able to make positive choices. Older preschool-aged kids are developing empathy, so they can now see how their actions might make a friend feel.

However, some preschool children may lag behind and continue to struggle with toddler-like behaviors. So remember to treat every child as an individual and give them a little more time and special guidance if needed. These kids may need developmental or behavioral evaluations and therapy, and you may need a parenting class to learn skills on how to manage their behaviors better. This was the case for our son.

When kids whine, nag, or cry, it's important for parents to use their skills to help their child build emotional control. We don't want to cause meltdown behaviors by being out of control ourselves or by giving attention to the unwanted behavior. You may recall that removing your attention, distracting a child, and redirecting a child work beautifully. And now that your preschool-aged child is more conversational, you should tell them that you don't understand what they're saying when they whine. Wait for them to speak correctly and calmly, and then respond.

Calming Skills for Preschoolers

When your child melts down, remind them to

- Take deep breaths and count to 10.
- Take a time-out to calm down.
- Use "I" statements (ie, "I feel sad when you take my toy. Please don't do that").
- Remind them to use their words.

As children start child care or gain siblings, conflict will arise with other kids. Continue to teach your child socially and emotionally to give them the skills they need to handle conflict peacefully and calm down when they become upset. Try a few of these skills when kids aren't getting along so well.

Conflict Resolution for Preschoolers

- Ask yourself whether they have the skills—language, social-emotional, and empathy skills.
- Handle the conflict as soon as possible (young children are "here and now" learners).
- Teach your child to set the rules of play from the beginning so everyone is on the same page. (This can help them avoid conflict.)
- Messages about keeping their hands to themselves and using kind words should be used consistently.
- It's important to teach children that games are not a competition (there is no first or best; everyone is awesome, and a game is just for fun).
- Model conflict resolution through stories, role-playing, puppets, kid shows, games, and other age-appropriate activities.
- Ask questions to help them solve problems—"Is it OK to . . . ? Do we . . . ? How do you feel when . . . ?"
- Teach them how to use "I" statements.
- Reward or praise negotiating, sharing, and taking turns.
- Facilitate apologies.

Problem-solving

When preschool-aged kids hit or act out aggressively, it's important to continue engaging them with critical thinking and problem-solving, not punishment. For example, if Brittany snatches a toy away from Joy and yells, "I want that one. Give it to me!" an appropriate response would be "Is it OK to snatch the toy, Brittany? You can ask Joy for a turn to play with the toy. But for now it's Joy's turn." Then give the toy back to Joy. And make sure to facilitate apologies too. Taking turns is an important message at every age.

Engaging critical thinking and problem-solving also works wonderfully when preschoolers refuse to follow instructions. Again, you want your child to adhere in this moment, but most importantly, you want them to eventually get it right on their own by using self-discipline. Make eye contact and give clear, step-by-step instructions. Next have your child repeat the instructions back to you. Give a time frame, or, better yet, set a timer. Be ready to praise your child for following instructions or to give consequences.

For example, when you ask Sammy to pick up his toys in the playroom, he pouts and refuses. An appropriate response would be "What time is it? It's cleanup time." Sammy should respond accordingly and start to pick up his toys. If he doesn't, you can say, "You have 5 minutes to pick up your toys, starting now, go! You can also try to make cleanup fun by offering to help or making it a race. Be sure to praise Sammy when he follows instructions and picks up his toys. If he continues to refuse, you can do so many things, because now you have all the pieces for this puzzle and "mad skills." Here are some suggestions to keep in your bag of tricks.

Nonadherence Bag of Tricks

- Leverage your loving relationship by sweetly saying something like "I thought you were my big girl helper" or "But you clean up so well" (another Jedi mind trick).
- Be childlike by making cleanup time a game or asking your child to show you how to clean up.
- Give a choice—for example, "Brush your teeth or I will do it for you" (most kids want to be independent).
- Use a verbal cue such as a countdown—5, 4, 3, 2, 1.
- Give positive reinforcement and make cleanup fun. You could discover who cleans the fastest, with the winner getting a sticker for their board.
- Use negative reinforcement: "Until you clean up these toys, you can't play with this one (their favorite)."
- Give consequences. Warn your child that they will lose their toy privilege if they don't clean up. Give them time to complete the task, but follow through with your warning if they do not adhere.
- Call a time-out. Kids often become upset when they don't want to follow instructions or are given consequences. If they melt down, call a time-out or give them some time to calm down. Then move forward with gaining adherence or giving consequences. Don't cave in just to keep the peace.

Now that you know what goes on in the minds of kids in early childhood and you can speak their language, you are better equipped to parent and discipline them appropriately. None of these skills that you learned about are magical, but they do work when used in a calm, consistent, instructive, and nurturing way. For those of you who have already survived this period, congratulations! But life is full of challenges: your little ones will grow up, and you will encounter more.

Parenting Prescription

Help your preschooler figure out their wonders, and get them kindergarten ready!

Chapter 8

School-age Period: 6 to 12 Years

Your child has now entered the age of reason. Oh my. During this stage, kids are growing by leaps and bounds in common sense, morals, and maturity. By this age, they will understand the difference between right and wrong and possess even more emotional self-control. But remember, each school-aged child is unique and widely varies in physical characteristics, mental capabilities, and social-emotional development.

Imagine visiting your child's elementary school. You head down the early elementary hallway, observing 6- and 7-year-old children who can sit and focus for 15 minutes. They are having concrete conversations and are working on their concern for others and control of their emotions. As you continue down the hallway, you also notice a group of 10- to 12-year-old kids hanging out. They look so grown-up. At this age, they are more abstract thinkers, capable of paying attention for longer periods of time, and totally focused on peer relationships. What a difference a couple of years can make in what your children learn, what you can expect of them, and how you should adjust your disciplinary strategies to help them make good decisions in life.

What Can My Child Do?

Use the following charts to gauge your child's development. Are they where they should be? Are your expectations appropriate?

> ### *What My Child Can Do: 6 to 9 Years*
>
> ☐ I can engage in conversations.
> ☐ I'm independent with most activities of daily living; I dress appropriately, prepare simple meals/snacks, and do chores.
> ☐ I can ride a bike, scooter, or skateboard.
> ☐ I have best friends.

(continued on next page)

☐ I'm concerned about fairness.

☐ I can consider "we" and show empathy toward others. Magical thinking is fading.

☐ I'm separate from my parents and family.

What My Child Can Do: 10 to 12 Years

☐ I'm focused on peer relationships.

☐ I may be experiencing peer pressure.

☐ I may be experiencing puberty (especially girls).

☐ I'm aware of body changes.

☐ I'm independent with activities of daily living.

☐ I have abstract thinking and know that death is irreversible.

☐ I'm developing racial identity.

What Does My Child Need From Me?

Allow Some Independence

School-aged kids are spending more and more time away from home. As they get older, more of their time is spent interacting with teachers and classmates, hanging out with friends, and engaging in various hobbies and extracurricular activities. So they really need to be ready for the world outside of your home.

During the school-age years, children are developing a sense of autonomy, or self-rule. Assist them by allowing them to make certain decisions for themselves, take charge of their personal belongings and hygiene, solve challenges, and share their thought process. Supporting your kids this way builds self-confidence and will help as they continue to learn in school, navigate social interactions, gain friends, and discover interests. It will also help them succeed outside the home and learn who they are, which helps strengthen their self-esteem.

Building Self-confidence and Self-esteem

Help your child build self-confidence by saying "I can" affirmations.

▶ I can do it.

▶ I can run fast.

▶ I can make a difference.

▶ I can get through this.

Self-confidence = "I can."

Help your child build self-esteem by saying "I am" affirmations.

- ▶ I am able to learn.
- ▶ I am kind.
- ▶ I am loved.

- ▶ I am enough.
- ▶ I am strong.

Self-esteem = "I love myself."

Friends will start to play an important part in your child's life. You'll learn a lot about what Susie said and what Susie thinks and what your daughter and Susie want to do when she comes over to visit. And as much as that seems wonderful, your daughter will face some challenges with friendships as well. She and Susie will fight, and your daughter's feelings will get hurt. Susie will have influence over her that you find unsettling. You can't solve all of her problems, but you can offer support and guidance by talking with her and by teaching her what healthy relationships look like, which will build her confidence and self-love, and by practicing with her conflict resolution and empathy skills. It also helps if you know that Susie's parents are like-minded and also teach Susie the same kind and positive lessons that you teach. Next time there is a school event, make sure to meet Susie's parents. It's a great way to help your child build positive friendships.

Did I mention that peer pressure starts around this time? Yikes! Know that when your child feels good about themselves, they'll be better able to resist negative peer pressure and make the right decisions for themselves. I'll stop right here for now, because we'll definitely take a deep dive into peer pressure in Chapter 9, Adolescence: 12 to 17 Years.

Parent From a Distance

Even though I just encouraged you to start cutting the cord, you still need to supervise, guide, and model behavior, but from a distance. The distance factor is key because school-aged children around 9 to 12 years old can get easily embarrassed and annoyed with "helicopter" parents in social spaces. Hovering around their friends is uncool. That's why you may notice your son disappears as soon as you arrive at the school function together and he avoids you like the plague the whole time. If you force a conversation, he may seem annoyed and bothered that you're talking with him in public or in front of his friends. So my advice is to get all the preparing done on the way there and debrief in the car on the way home. Sit back and watch. If your child needs you, they know where you are. If you need to speak with your child during an event, call them over and speak privately. The good news is that school-aged kids are exact opposites at home. They still want your attention, still need quality time, and even try to sleep in your bed. So that cord? It's more like a detachable cord.

Check in with your child each day to ask how they are doing or feeling. Remind them that you are always available to talk about anything. Know that your child may seem more interested in what their friends say, but they still need you. Continue to build a positive relationship, so they feel comfortable coming to you. Set aside uninterrupted quality time; have fun together; and chat about their interests, even if those are boring to you (eg, video games, sports, latest fashion trends, and TV shows).

Recognize if your child is having difficulty navigating this period, whether in academics, friendships, emotions, or bullying. More on that later. These challenges can harm the development of "selfie" skills if not recognized and managed appropriately. Build a support system to form a safety net around your child, and be involved at their school. Get to know the teacher, principal, and counselors. Visit, call, or email them to keep the "line of communication" open and address any problems academically or behaviorally. Request a team meeting with the teacher and/or other school personnel to brainstorm ways to meet the needs of your child and implement a plan of action. Involve your pediatrician, who can guide you as a parent and advocate for your child separately from the school system.

Why Does My Child Do That, and What Can I Do About It?

School-aged children are still concrete, literal thinkers but are now adding logical thought processes. So if you're speaking in hypotheticals, school-aged kids aren't likely to understand. This lack of figurative thinking is also why elementary kids aren't great liars and easily get caught in a lie. They just can't do the mental gymnastics to weave a tale and maintain it—yet. However, some children as early as 8 years old start to back up their lies and judge the lies of others.

Thankfully, egocentrism is also fading away (disclaimer: even some adults still have a little). Now your children can consider what other people may be feeling and thinking. And they also realize that their thoughts and feelings may differ from those of others. You may be hearing "That's my opinion" or "What do you think?"

Here are classic behavior concerns in school-aged kids.

Lying

Kids start to lie as early as 3 years old when they figure out you aren't ever-present and all-knowing. Kids 4 or 5 years old know that telling a lie is wrong. Between 5 and 8 years, kids fib a lot to get away with doing things they shouldn't do or to test the limits of what they can get away with saying or doing. Yet, they will often fess up when questioned, because they are easily caught in the lie or find it difficult to maintain the lie. Unfortunately, as kids get older, they get better at telling lies and sticking to them. Lies can range from making up imaginative stories (preschoolers) to either faking it in order to impress someone or creating a tall tale for the teacher, like "My dog ate my homework," in order to escape blame (middle schoolers).

Although lying is frowned on, it's a part of children's emotional and intellectual development. And since all children lie at one time or another, don't worry that you have a pathological liar on your hands. Stay calm and prepare for this developmental stage. To curb lying in school-aged kids, it's important to understand why they lie or what they gain from lying and address the behavior appropriately.

Common Reasons Why Kids Lie

- To feel better about themselves
- To gain approval of their peers and to fit in
- To compete with their peers and seem better than others
- To deflect focus elsewhere
- Because they watch you do it and get away with it
- Because they honestly forgot
- To get attention
- Because they are speaking before thinking (impulsive lying)
- To test limits
- To keep out of trouble

Handling Lying

- Consider how often the child does it and to what degree.
- Occasional white lies can be ignored, or you can redirect your child to the facts by asking, for example, "Did she really hit you on purpose, or did you get hit by accident?"
- Give them a chance to tell the truth. You can ask something like "Is that true or are you telling a story? Tell me what happened again." Give them 5 to 10 seconds to process and answer.
- Don't forget to stay calm and praise children for telling the truth by saying, for example, "Thanks for telling Mom (or Dad) the truth."
- Repetitive, harmful lying should have consequences to teach the child that lying is unacceptable.

Encourage responsibility by stressing the importance of telling the truth and by addressing the reason for the lie (eg, lying about doing schoolwork). In that case, the child should still have to complete the work even if it's too late to turn the work in (logical consequence) and will likely get a poor grade on that assignment (natural consequence). You should brainstorm ways to complete homework in a timely manner. Other reasonable consequences may include loss of privileges, such as taking away the phone or video games.

Notice that none of my advice includes calling your child a liar or yelling at, threatening, shaming, or hitting them or any other forms of harmful behavior. If you call your child a liar today, will they always be a liar? No. They lied. That's it. Label the behavior, not the child!

Anger, Talking Back, and Disrespect

The most basic human emotions are happiness, sadness, anger, and fear. Anger is a normal human emotion. It's not a negative emotion and shouldn't be frowned on. When a child feels anger, a behavior follows. It can be a positive response that communicates the seriousness of a problem and also helps motivate the child to act and solve the problem.

However, negative responses to anger can be harmful. In school-aged children and adolescents, anger can manifest in various ways, such as shutting down, being irritable, talking back, arguing, refusing to follow instructions, fighting, or raging.

Parents and other caregivers should try to understand the source of a child's anger and teach them productive ways to handle frustrations. Kids act out what they can't talk out. In Chapter 10, Be Aware: From ACEs to Healing, we'll talk about the developing brain of a child. Children have an underdeveloped "thinking brain" (prefrontal cortex), which has less control over the "primitive brain" (amygdala) that triggers the fight, flight, or freeze response when provoked. Although these behaviors are disturbing, when kids act out of anger they are communicating something. For example,

- An unmet need (eg, there is a lack of attention or support, the child is feeling hungry or tired)
- A great loss (eg, death of a close family member, divorce, relocating)
- A traumatic experience (eg, abuse, bullying)
- A dysfunctional environment (eg, domestic violence, community violence)
- A medical, mental health, or learning problem (eg, puberty, depression, dyslexia, attention-deficit/hyperactivity disorder)

So get to the root of the anger and heal from there. I heard an anger management specialist once say, "You have to meet the need before you can plant a seed."

When kids give attitude, get sassy, or act downright disrespectful, it may be hard to focus on the child's needs. Your buttons have been pushed, and you may be well on your way to behaving in kind. Recall that you are the model and fully equipped to take a deep breath, calm down, and use your positive parenting skills. So just woosah!

Here is how to handle kids' anger, talking back, and disrespect.

Emotion Coaching

Emotion coaching is a parenting technique that helps kids understand their feelings and respond in healthy ways. It is important for parents to teach kids how to cope with emotions so they can self-regulate, be confident, build healthy relationships, and navigate life's challenges. According to The Gottman Institute, there are 5 steps to emotion coaching. Notice how the mom and son work through homework battles in the following scenario:

Step 1. Observe your child's emotion (this is also the perfect time to calm yourself down).

Mom: Sam, you seem upset. Are you having trouble with your schoolwork?

Step 2. Allow your child to express their emotions. Focus on how to connect and teach during this moment. Try not to control or dismiss your child's thoughts. Resist the urge to tell your child to suck up their emotions. For example, don't say, "Big girls don't cry," or "Be a man."

Sam: I can't do it! It doesn't make any sense. I need help.

Step 3. Listen to your child, and try to understand their point of view. Support your child's feelings (don't judge or criticize).

Mom: Sam, I hear you.

Step 4. Help your child name emotions ("You look angry" or "You can say, 'I feel mad'"). Also, help children name more abstract emotions, like "frustrated," "confused," or "disappointed."

Mom: I know it can be frustrating when something is hard to understand.

Step 5. Solve the problem together, but use disciplinary skills to handle misbehavior.

Mom: What can you do to help yourself when you feel this way?

Sam: I can take a break. Oh, and ask for help.

Mom: Good, because sitting in here, feeling frustrated, doesn't help you get your homework done. You can also google this type of problem and watch a video on how to solve it. Since I am here now, I can try to help. But you have to keep your cool. OK?

Sam: Thanks, Mom. I'll try.

Now if your child has a meltdown or some other misbehavior while you are helping them with their math homework, you'll have plenty of positive parenting skills to manage the situation.

Other Anger Management Tips

- Avoid triggers—predict, plan, prepare.
- Don't compare kids.
- Be fair.
- Try not to embarrass.
- Manage your expectations.
- Tell social stories.
- Prompt calming skills.
- Allow exploration or experimentation.
- Model calming techniques—continued from preschool age.
- Explain the situation.
- Give options.
- Make things fun.
- Praise along the way.
- Practice positive self-talk.
- Encourage prosocial activities to enhance social-emotional skills (eg, sports, community service, summer programs).
- Give the child a minute (patience).

Sometimes anger can get out of hand. In severe cases, when lives are potentially in danger, you may need to call 911. Specifically ask for the mental health police unit. In the state of Florida, we have access to the mobile crisis unit by calling 211. Specially trained officers and mental health specialists will come to help manage the situation. However, earlier recognition is crucial when anger needs intervention. Discuss it with your pediatrician or your child's school counselor. Connect with your child and engage them in mindfulness practices such as exercise, adequate sleep, meditation, and yoga. Get help if your child exhibits any of the following anger warning signs:

- Has difficulty controlling aggressive impulses
- Is always angry and has frequent, explosive tantrums
- Consistently reacts with opposition
- Blames others for their wrongdoings
- Has difficulty maintaining friendships because of conflict
- Is focused on payback
- Makes suicidal or homicidal threats or attempts
- Destroys property
- Often expresses hate
- Hurts animals or small children

Having a home safety plan for children who struggle with anger is very important. You or any caregiver should know whom to call, where to go, and what to do in a behavior emergency. Your pediatrician, child's therapist, or child's psychiatrist can help put the plan together. Also, make sure to lock up weapons and secure potentially harmful items in the home.

Sibling Rivalry

Get 2 or more kids in a room together and there will be conflict. So it's no surprise that siblings who spend most of their time together will have conflict as well. The yelling—"Leave me alone! Stop it! Mom!"—and tension can be very frustrating and distressing to parents. Parents long for ways not only to manage sibling conflict peacefully and positively but also to teach children how to handle conflict with siblings among themselves. Sibling rivalry goes beyond sibling conflict and can encompass physical fighting, jealousy, and competition. However, stay hopeful, because most kids "love on" each other just as much as they fight, and they grow to be very close to their siblings despite the fighting when they were young.

Understanding Sibling Rivalry

Understanding why siblings fight can help you identify ways to reduce the drama. Sibling rivalry occurs because

- Children lack conflict resolution skills or they may be handling conflict as their parents do.
- Siblings see each other as competitors for their parents' time, attention, and love.
- Older siblings are often jealous of a new sibling. The older sibling feels as if they have been replaced or pushed to the side when the younger child shows up and gets more attention.
- As younger siblings grow up and fight for independence, they no longer accept the older sibling's rule.

Helping Siblings Get Along Better

By teaching children how to handle conflict, reducing competition, and adequately paying attention to everyone, parents can help them get along better.

- Model peace, kindness, and calmness in your home.
- Teach aged-based conflict resolution skills through stories, role-playing, modeling, and other age-appropriate activities.

- Don't label or compare your kids (eg, "My sweet one" or "Be more like Jim").
- Set aside quality time for each child (eg, "Brandon's time").
- Provide private space and private activities for each child (eg, a kid cave, "me time," or a playdate alone with school friends).
- As much as possible, stay out of the fight and let them work it out (eg, "Do I need to come in there?" or "I hear a lot of loud noise. Is everything OK in there?").
- If it escalates or becomes dangerous, separate the children and talk with them individually.
- Try not to take sides. A fight usually "takes two to tango."
- Emphasize life skills (eg, compromise and negotiation).
- Give fair consequences (eg, removing a toy that siblings aren't sharing nicely).
- Make a schedule (eg, Ken's video game time, Mary's TV time, or Tim's computer time).
- Require apologies and move on.
- Praise or reward sibling love, peace, and cooperation.

In some cases, sibling rivalry can be severe. It can create family dysfunction and threaten the whole family's physical, emotional, and psychological health. If this is your situation, seek the help of your pediatrician, a family mental health counselor, a behavioral interventionist, or combined services. Especially if the dynamics are causing marital problems, physical harm, or mental impairment, such as rage, anxiety, or depression.

Now you speak "middle childhood"! You may be a little rusty and make some communication errors, but you are so much closer to understanding, connecting, and working with your child in a positive way. Your next adventure awaits as we head out into the final frontier—adolescence!

Let us pray!

Parenting Prescription

Support your school-aged child in becoming more independent and responsible. Practice emotion coaching to manage your child's anger.

Chapter 9

Adolescence: 12 to 17 Years

I love teenagers! They are so cool; I live vicariously through them. You know, the iconic teen: eyes glued to their iPhone, fingers texting at lightning speed, and head bobbing to the beat in their AirPods. Without a care in the world, so it seems. But in all honesty, this period is challenging for both parents and teens. Parents worry about the future and whether their teen is ready to make it on their own. And even though it may not be obvious, teens also worry about school performance, relationships, body image, family life—the list goes on and on. In fact, a 2019 Pew Research Center survey of US teens aged 13 to 17 years showed that adolescents see anxiety and depression as a top issue among their peers.

I know teenagers look, act, and sometimes even think that they are adults. But remember, the adolescent brain is not yet physically matured. In fact, the prefrontal cortex (or thinking and reasoning part of the brain) is not fully developed until around the age of 24 years. More on this later. . . .

What Can My Teen Do?

Use the following charts to gauge your teen's development. Are they where they should be? Are your expectations appropriate?

What My Teen Can Do: 12 to 14 Years

- ☐ I am experiencing puberty (earlier for girls).
- ☐ I am more concerned about my looks.
- ☐ I care about what my friends think.
- ☐ I may be pulling away from my parents.
- ☐ I am more stressed with schoolwork.
- ☐ I care about right and wrong.

(continued on next page)

☐ I am better at talking through my feelings.

☐ I am beginning to understand the effects of my actions (abstract thinking). I can engage in hypothetical conversations and discuss moral judgment.

What My Teen Can Do: 15 to 17 Years

☐ Romantic relationships take center stage.

☐ Girls reach pubertal maturation, but boys continue to grow until young adulthood.

☐ Body image issues can lead to self-esteem issues and eating disorders.

☐ Stressors can lead to depression and anxiety.

☐ I may engage in risky behaviors—for example, drugs, sex, feeling "invincible."

☐ I am preparing for adulthood—for example, getting a job, going to college, leaving home.

☐ I am more capable of reasoning through choices and consequences.

☐ I have my own unique personality and beliefs.

☐ I am beginning to think long term and set goals.

What Does My Teen Need From Me?

Now more than ever, adolescents need caregivers to listen to their point of view and try to understand the changes and challenges that come with the teenage years. They would also like for us to treat them like an adult, unless, of course, it's time to pay for something or solve a major problem. If you're feeling used as a parent, you're not alone. We have our work cut out for us in mastering these mixed messages from our teens. To help our teens rock adolescence, we must have open and honest dialogue, celebrate who they are, and start teaching them how to think like an adult.

Keep It Real

Adolescence is full of physical, mental, and social changes. Therefore, I can't express enough how important it is for caregivers to prepare teens on how to navigate through these ever-changing times. *Menstrual period. Emotional overload. Body odor. Braces. Acne. Self-esteem issues. Boyfriends. Sexual orientation. Girlfriends. Sex. Friends and enemies. Dating. Popularity. Social media. Cyberbullying. Gaming. Drugs. Alcohol. Vaping. Tattoos. Piercings. Jobs. Driving. Schoolwork. College. Extracurricular activities. Dreams. Family life. Police encounters. Racism. Stress. Anxiety. Depression. Suicide. Adversity.*

All of these require parents to engage in real talk with their teens. You want your teenager to learn from you first and foremost and not from incorrect and harmful information from friends. I can't count the number of times I've had to explain pubertal body changes to a preteen because their parent was too uncomfortable or not ready to have that conversation. Or how many times I've had to correct "they say" misinformation. Don't get me wrong! As a pediatrician, I value having difficult conversations with teens, but parents should also be having them. Nothing should be off the table when it comes to telling your teen what's out there in the world and how best to handle it to protect themselves.

Get creative. Dissect that TikTok post, movie scene, or music video together. Read age-specific books on puberty together. Ask, "Do you like boys, girls, both, or neither romantically?" to spark conversation around sexuality. Pull up age-appropriate sexually transmitted infection graphics from the Centers for Disease Control and Prevention website to aid in your conversation. Explore your teen's feelings around racism and instances of police brutality. Engage in real-life scenarios to assess how teens will handle being in situations of texting while driving, being offered drugs or alcohol, the tempting behaviors on social media, or any dating violence. Help your teen develop positive coping strategies to manage these situations and to manage the stressors of academic demands and other personal obstacles.

Now the real challenge is getting teens to accept our guidance, because they already know it all (or so they think). But just know that you still have so much to offer your teen, and as much as they resist your advice, they know you care. Whether they like it or not, have frequent conversations about the following common adolescent challenges:

- Early introduction to puberty and sex education is important. Discuss puberty before it occurs.
- Help your child understand that body and emotional changes are a typical part of growing up and they are not alone.
- Discuss expected behaviors and social boundaries with your child.
- Visit trusted resources together, such as https://amaze.org.
- Inquire about sexuality.
- Discuss your family's beliefs, expectations, and key considerations about sex. To help frame conversations, read *There's No Place Like Home . . . for Sex Education* by Mary Gossart.
- Discuss what makes relationships healthy and what to do when they are not.
- Explain consent and how to make sure you have it.

- Plan for difficult or uncomfortable situations. Ask them what they would do if
  — They're at a party with friends and drugs are being used.
  — They're in a car with someone who's drinking or texting while driving.
  — Their boyfriend or girlfriend or partner wants them to have sex and they're not ready.
- Ask whether they're experiencing any stress, anxiety, or depression and/or they're having suicidal thoughts. (Monitor for signs, described later on this page.)
- Stress the importance of a healthy lifestyle and adequate sleep.
- Educate them on how media can negatively affect body image and self-esteem and ways to use it appropriately.
- Discuss how excessive gaming can be harmful and ways to limit overexposure. Visit www.commonsensemedia.org or create a family media use plan at www.healthychildren.org/English/media.
- Brainstorm positive coping strategies for scenarios such as peer pressure, bullying, and academic stress.

Know the Signs

Here are the signs of depression and risk for suicide.

- ▶ Feelings of hopelessness, helplessness, and sadness
- ▶ Taking actions that are risky
- ▶ Change in behavior
- ▶ Threats or thoughts of harming oneself
- ▶ Situations of sudden trauma or loss

If your teen has any of these symptoms, call the National Suicide Prevention Lifeline at 800/273-8255 for help. Other mental health concerns may arise during adolescence. Visit https://mentalhealthliteracy.org for additional information.

Having these ongoing conversations strengthens the parent-teen bond, trust, and mutual respect and is an integral part of discipline that makes it easier to instruct and correct teens when they make a mistake.

See Them

One of my favorite movies of all time, *Avatar*, uses the phrase "I see you" to symbolize how crucial it is to unconditionally "see" each other on a deeper level. To see the love, understand the feelings, and connect to the soul of another. When you send the message "I see you" to your teen, you communicate that you see the best in them and they mean the world to you. A teen who truly feels seen will, in turn, trust and follow your leadership, overcome any challenges, and flourish in life.

How do you tell your child, "I see you"? (Remember, actions speak louder than words.)

- Accept their individuality (accepting it doesn't mean you necessarily agree with all of their choices).
- Respect their individual choices and opinions, as long as they are safe.
- Listen and try to understand their feelings.
- Show interest in their hobbies, and show up for their activities.
- Compliment their efforts and accomplishments.
- Express love and affection—find their love language and learn to speak it (see Chapter 2, A Win-Win Approach: The High Five Essentials of Effective and Positive Parenting).
- Spend time together, and get to know each other better.

Adult Practice

I'm always asking teens, "What are you going to do when you grow up? How do you help your family currently? What are you doing with yourself this summer? Are you getting a job?" I make it my business to stimulate their independent thought processes and to gauge their readiness for life on their own.

Parents should also prompt these conversations often, and they should help teens move successfully into young adulthood by

- Providing a stepwise approach to independence
- Allowing privacy within limits
- Encouraging employment or other prosocial activities (eg, community or religious service)
- Teaching money management
- Assigning roles contributing to the family or household
- Prompting appropriate decision-making and goal setting
- Challenging poor choices
- Offering support when necessary and especially when requested
- Promoting self-care and healthy practices

Why Does My Teen Do That, and What Can I Do About It?

Attitude and Risky Behavior

Even though some kids start puberty during the school-age years, the hallmark of adolescence is puberty. The physical and emotional changes of puberty result from hormonal changes in the body and ongoing brain development. Hormones can make us all do and say some unusual things! Their effect is no different for kids going through puberty.

Teens have bad attitudes from time to time (or minute to minute). Knowing that attitude and rebellion are driven by hormonal changes makes it easier to not take the drama personally. It should also be comforting to know that it will pass as long as you manage the behaviors appropriately. It starts with you, the parent, dealing with the teenage years in a peaceful, positive, and skillful way. When your teen yells, insults you, slams doors, and refuses to do what you ask, model keeping your cool, using your words to express what you are noticing and feeling, and firmly stating your expectations, limits, and consequences as needed. If your teen seems withdrawn or self-isolated and all attempts to chat have failed, set up an activity they love in order to reconnect and increase the chance of their opening up. No matter what, continue to tell teens how much you love them and want the best for them. And by all means, show them what you want their behavior to be.

We mentioned earlier that the adolescent brain is still maturing. This includes the thinking/reasoning part of the brain, or the prefrontal cortex. However, the amygdala, or emotional center of the brain, is fully functional much earlier. Neuroscientists believe that this brain maturity mismatch can explain most adolescent behavior and why teens seem to be so driven by emotions and to impulsively throw caution to the wind.

For example, if you ask a teen whether trying drugs is a positive choice, he'll surely say, "No!" Most of the time, when tempted, he'll use good judgment and decide not to use drugs. However, he may encounter a situation when all of his friends and the girl he's "crushing on" coax him to just give drugs a try. Many teens in a split second might go along with the pleading of cheering peers. Darn amygdala!

The proverbial angel on one shoulder and devil on the other also cause teens to rationalize in weird ways and take risk.

They can think abstractly but sometimes miss the big picture because impulsive urges cloud their judgment, giving them a false sense of invincibility. I've heard teenagers give the most irrational explanations for dangerous behaviors: "But everybody's doing it." "I don't know anyone that happened to." "One time won't hurt." "I won't get caught." "I'm not worried about it." "I don't need a condom, because I'm the only one."

Here are some strategies to equip teens to think more clearly in the moment.

- Monitor behavior, friends, relationships, and habits and discuss what you notice.
- Raise awareness or join a cause together.
- Review the facts.
- Set clear expectations and rules. Allow teen participation and compromise when possible.

- Your teen can earn privileges and more independence by making positive choices.
- Implement an honesty policy.
- Think like a teen and be proactive with parental control apps and a safety contract.

These scenarios play out over and over again in the lives of adolescents. The good news is that the prefrontal cortex eventually catches up and begins to manage the amygdala. And again, caregivers are instrumental in supporting teens in making split-second, good decisions.

Rebellion

Teenage rebellion is all about the struggle for independence and freedom to do as one pleases. The teenage period is sometimes called the *age of consent* for that reason, because teens want to have the final say in what they do. Teens often question authority and the value of societal norms, such as the importance of educational attainment, cleanliness, being dependable, and setting life goals. They don't recognize the value when they aren't interested.

Adolescents also beg to do the next big thing even when we don't think they're quite ready. They may ask,

- When can I start driving?
- When can I wear makeup?
- When can I go on my first date?
- Why do I need to go to bed or have time limits on my phone and games?
- When can I get a job and have my own money to do with as I please?

Parents must gradually allow opportunities for more independence over time as their teenager handles responsibilities appropriately. Once they show themselves to be trustworthy, you can give them more freedom. I often see kids doing things and having privileges they're clearly unready for—don't allow your teen to move too fast.

That said, be prepared to handle poor choices as your teen gains more freedom. For teens who consistently text while driving despite being told the dangers of doing so, who disregard curfew and come home drunk and smelling of marijuana, who fail a class because they'd rather play video games, or who go viral for a sexually explicit post, it's time for some tough love. These behaviors are immature and harmful and shouldn't be rewarded with being able to drive a car, go out on the weekend, or own a game console or social media account. Again, discipline is not about punishing negative behavior. It's about your teen being safe, upholding expectations, taking responsibility for choices, and accepting consequences for their actions. Teens get to choose their actions, and parents get to respond to those choices by holding teens accountable.

Peer Pressure and Toxic Relationships

We mentioned earlier that as teens struggle to be independent, they pull away from their family unit, and peer relationships take center stage. Teens often say that their friends listen, understand, and accept them more than their parents do. Therefore, teens are more likely to follow peer persuasion than the counsel of their parents.

Being accepted socially is another main concern of teenagers. Note how your teen adjusts their clothing, hair, slang, and musical style to fit in or even impress their peers. This behavior can be worrisome for parents when they see their teenager exhibit follower behavior, especially if they're doing inappropriate things or hanging out with the wrong crowd. Caregivers really need to monitor adolescent relationships, whether romantic or platonic, to ensure parental guidance, as needed.

I know you're wondering whether you have a fighting chance against peer pressure. Well, if you've already been doing most of what's in this book, your chance is excellent! If not, you have some work to do. It's never too late to improve your influence with your child.

First, telling your teen what not to do isn't very effective, like the talk about "sex, drugs, and hip-hop" (nobody says "rock 'n' roll" anymore). "Don't have sex. Don't do drugs. Don't smoke and don't drink alcohol. That music you listen to makes you want to have sex, so don't listen to it either. If you get pregnant, you've got to leave and care for your own child. If you go to jail, I'm not coming to get you. Got it? That's all." Again, evidence shows this doesn't work.

Second, break the talk up into multiple conversations. Don't teach them everything at once or they'll probably be overwhelmed, shut down, and unlikely to remember anything you said. Use books, online resources, and content that is popular with teens as a guide or starting point. Stay current, people!

Third, speak their language. Teens are smart, nearing adulthood, and wanting to be treated in kind. They want an explanation and want to have their say in the matter. So listen and educate them on how sex, drugs, and media can affect their life. Present these as choices (which they really are) and why they should choose wisely. Explain the consequences of engaging in adult behaviors without adult resources. Be honest about your experiences when you were their age. They may throw these in your face later, but your early mistakes are still valuable teachable moments.

Last, through casual conversations with your teen, encourage them to brainstorm ways around peer pressure, while still maintaining their "swag." I love the idea of having a distress code for when your teen needs a way out of an uncomfortable situation, such as texting a certain emoji or word. It alerts the parent to call the teen and tell them to come home immediately for some emergency. This puts the blame on the parent, so the teen won't take the "L" (loss). Although teens need to be OK with saying no, having multiple layers of protection is best.

Another aspect of peer relationships in adolescence is dating. The same considerations apply when we are discussing romantic relationships with teens. However, the particulars of dating violence should be covered as well. Make sure your own relationships show your teen what healthy relationships look like. And if that's a struggle, be transparent with your teen about the unhealthy aspects and how you plan to improve your situation.

"First love" often happens in adolescence. Teens fall head over heels in love, become inseparable, and plan for their future together. But in most cases, forever never happens and, instead, heartbreak occurs. Love loss is a part of growing up. It hurts and is especially painful for a parent to watch. Just know your teenager will get through it with your support.

What worries me more is when teen relationships become abusive. Teens who have been exposed to family domestic violence, who have been harshly disciplined, or who struggle with low self-esteem, mental illness, or addiction are more at risk for dating violence. When teens have been exposed to violence, dating violence may feel normal. But it's not! Impress upon your teen that real love doesn't hurt.

So keep an eye on your teen's relationships with friends and love interests to ensure they aren't toxic and to intervene on their behalf sooner rather than later. Hopefully you recall that one major element of the positive parenting puzzle is Good Relational Health Between Parent and Child. Puzzle pieces like **love and affection, honesty, respect, connection, belonging, support, and a friendly relationship** all fit together to create a healthy relationship between a parent and teen. Those same principles apply for your teen's peer relationships to be healthy.

Teaching teenagers the signs of an unhealthy relationship is key. In addition, supporting them to end a toxic relationship is critical for their safety and well-being. Your teen may disagree that their crew is trouble and leading them down the wrong path. You may need to gather the support of others they trust—a teacher, family member, mentor, or pediatrician—to help them understand that their friend or partner isn't good for them and why. Explain to your teen that their primary responsibility is to love and care for themselves and not to compromise themselves for someone else.

Signs of an unhealthy or toxic teen relationship are

- Jealousy or lack of trust
- Can't be yourself

- Can't do things separately or have different interests
- Insulting, mean, condescending, or derogatory comments (verbal abuse)
- Hitting, pushing, choking, or grabbing the other (physical abuse)
- Controlling, bullying, passive-aggressive, or isolating behaviors (emotional abuse)
- Blame and shame
- Constant arguing or always feeling angry
- Pushing or forcing sex or having pushed or forced sex, using drugs, or participating in risky behavior that you're uncomfortable doing
- Breaking rules or committing crimes
- Becoming someone you don't recognize or like

Your teen may need help ending a toxic relationship. Here's how to help.

- Talk it out.
- Help them weigh pros and cons.
- Convince them to take a break or cease all communication for a period of time.
- Have a family intervention to help run interference.
- Find or create a support group.
- Get them counseling.
- If safety is a concern, parents need to get involved, or parents need to get a restraining order, call the National Teen Dating Abuse Helpline 24/7 at 866/331-9474 or go to www.loveisrespect.org.

For you and your teen to survive adolescence, you must understand what your teen is going through (surely, you haven't forgotten); set realistic expectations; and respond empathically. You must continue to build a positive parent-teen relationship. You must use effective parenting strategies that encourage appropriate choices and correct unwanted behaviors. And finally, you must anticipate your teen's environment to prepare for the pitfalls they will face. Consistently and lovingly use the High Five Essentials and watch your teen soar!

Parenting Prescription

▶ Empathize through puberty.

▶ Monitor and guide peer relationships.

▶ Allow earned, stepwise independence and responsibility.

Chapter 10

Be Aware: From ACEs to Healing— Building Resilience and Beyond

One morning, nearly 6 years ago, as I drove to work and listened to a favorite radio talk show, a doctor called in to correct and inform the commentary. Adiaha Spinks-Franklin, MD, a behavioral pediatrician, explained adverse childhood experiences (ACEs) and the connection between childhood trauma, toxic stress, and poor physical, mental, and behavioral health outcomes that could affect an individual for a lifetime.

What she said was so profound that I dived into the literature and began to educate myself about ACEs. I also tracked her down and invited her to be a guest on my podcast, *KIDing Around with Dr. Candice*. (Take a listen to episode 31.)

What Are ACEs?

Dr Spinks-Franklin explained that ACEs are negative experiences people have during childhood that can have long-term consequences on their development, behavior, and health well into adulthood. ACEs fall into 3 categories: abuse, neglect, and family dysfunction. Abuse includes physical, emotional, and sexual abuse. Neglect is emotional and physical neglect. Household dysfunction includes

- Parental separation and divorce
- Living in a household with an adult with an untreated mental illness or a substance use problem
- Witnessing domestic violence
- Death of a parent
- Having an incarcerated parent or other caregiver
- Being in foster care

There are more ACEs beyond the original 10. Immigration, war, natural disasters, death of a loved one, bullying, dating violence, and many others are all adversities that can harm the developing brains and bodies of young people. Another consideration is the impact of ACEs on communities. ACEs don't discriminate; they affect us all. But individuals in underserved communities may have higher doses of ACEs due to the added toxic stress of poverty, violence, discrimination, lack of resources, and other community-wide trauma. Wendy Ellis, DrPH, MPH, calls it "The Pair of Aces," shown in the following figure. These adverse community environments create the toxic roots that put kids in harm's way of childhood trauma. In these children, we can note poorer school performance and worse physical, psychological, and behavioral health outcomes.

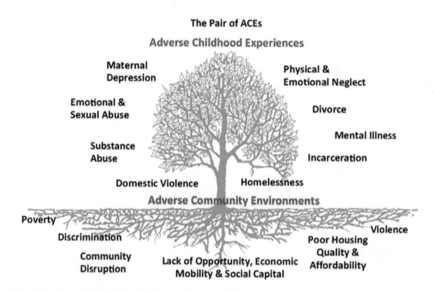

Reproduced from Ellis WR, Dietz WH. A new framework for addressing adverse childhood and community experiences: the building community resilience model. *Acad Pediatr.* 2017;17(7S):S86–S93.

History of ACEs

The original Adverse Childhood Experiences Study in 1998 was a partnership between Kaiser Permanente and the Centers for Disease Control and Prevention, authored by Vincent Felitti, MD, and Robert Anda, MD. The study participants included more than 17,000 mostly educated, insured, white, middle to upper class adult patients from San Diego County, CA. The landmark study showed that 67% of the population had at least one ACE and 13% of the population had 4 or more. It also showed that the more ACEs you have, the more potential for negative health outcomes. Since that study, research around ACEs has exploded, with every major academic center studying their effects on our lives and proposing ways to treat them. One such pioneer, Nadine Burke Harris, MD, MPH, FAAP, pediatrician and first Surgeon General of California, has called for universal ACEs screening and is currently making it happen with pediatricians in California. I recommend you read her book *The Deepest Well* and look at the work of the Center for Youth Wellness, which she cofounded.

ACEs Are Common

Dr Spinks-Franklin says, in the United States, by the age of 8 years, 1 in 3 children has at least one ACE; by adolescence, one-half; and by adulthood, 2 out of 3. The more ACEs a person has, the greater their risk for serious developmental disabilities, behavior disorders, and chronic medical conditions, such as heart disease, stroke, and cancer.

Toxic Stress and the Stress Response System

Dr Spinks-Franklin goes on to explain the connection between childhood trauma and adverse health and well-being. The mediator is toxic stress. Not all stress is bad stress. There are 3 levels of stress that science has described: positive, tolerable, and toxic stress.

- **Positive stress** refers to a temporarily stressful event that is positive overall. It causes a temporary increase of stress hormones, but they go completely back to normal once the stressful event ends (eg, first day at a new school, getting immunizations, or performing for a crowd).
- **Tolerable stress** is a circumstance in which a person experiences a traumatic event but their family members are there to buffer them through the experience and protect and guide them. So their body stress hormone levels go up, and stay up temporarily, but eventually come back down to normal without many long-term consequences, because their family helped protect them, helped them recover, and helped them overcome that toxic experience. That could be surviving a house fire, experiencing a natural disaster, or one of the known ACEs, such as witnessing domestic violence, having a parent who is incarcerated, or experiencing abuse.
- **Toxic stress** occurs when a child experiences a traumatic event but doesn't have a support system or buffer to help them get through it. The body's stress hormone levels stay high for months or years at a time. It's that toxic level of stress that causes damage to the organs, nervous system in the brain, immune system, hormonal system, and even our DNA.

Lions, tigers, and bears are one thing, but here in Florida, we have to worry about alligators, bears, and sharks. So when my family goes out into nature, I'm always on high alert. Imagine splashing around in the warm waters off Clearwater Beach. You're about waist deep with the kids close by when someone yells, "Shark!" (Remember the "duh nah, duh nah, duh nah" music from *Jaws*?)

In a split second, the stress response system goes into action. The amygdala, the emotional center of the brain, detects danger and alerts the hypothalamus to wake up the pituitary gland, which in turn signals the adrenal glands. The hypothalamic-pituitary-adrenal, or HPA, axis is like a domino effect ending with the release of cortisol and adrenaline, 2 of the body's key stress hormones. Cortisol travels through the bloodstream to other body parts, signaling them to also react to the shark. As a result, you fight, flee, or freeze.

Hopefully, there really isn't a shark or there's just a little one who swims away in the frenzy of people screaming and fleeing the waters. As you lie on the beach, clutching your kids with your heart pounding in your chest, the prefrontal cortex (the thinking and reasoning part of the brain) slowly takes control and helps you recognize safety and calm down. It alerts all the other players to reverse course, allowing the stress hormones to come back to baseline. Whew!

Now imagine children who have constant "sharks" in their lives and no one to save them. They are dealing with a parent with mental illness, being sexually abused, living in the foster care system, or facing discrimination. For these

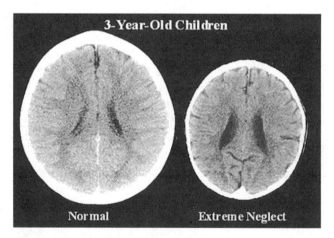

Abnormal brain development following sensory-deprivation neglect in early childhood. Left, CT (computed tomographic) scan of a healthy 3-year-old with an average head size. Right, CT scan of a 3-year-old with severe sensory-deprivation neglect; this child's brain is significantly smaller and has enlarged ventricles and cortical atrophy.
© 1997 Bruce D. Perry, MD, PhD, ChildTrauma Academy.

children, the stress response system can become overactive and dysregulated and can lead to a child who responds to and deals with stress dysfunctionally.

The hippocampus (the learning and memory center of the brain) and the frontal lobe (the mission control center of the brain) become smaller in size under toxic stress. Therefore, the brain has trouble thinking and solving problems, having self-control, learning new information, and remembering what is already learned. On the other hand, the amygdala gets larger in size. It surveys for danger constantly even when there is none. The lower, more primitive brain takes over and the upper, reasoning brain goes off-line. So you have a child who can be triggered by anything that then sets off their stress response. They're going to fight, fly, or shut down. Some parents (and teachers) wonder whether a kid has attention-deficit/hyperactivity disorder (ADHD), when actually this child is experiencing stress responses due to trauma in their life. It isn't ADHD. It's symptoms of toxic stress.

"Bad Kids" or Traumatized Kids?

Kids acting out are not necessarily "bad kids." Remember, they act out what they can't talk about. We have to look deeper into what's going on with them and their home life. According to Dr Spinks-Franklin, behavior is a form of communication and it has meaning. It's important for us to realize that when we encounter children misbehaving, they're actually trying to tell us something. We shouldn't be so quick to label them as "bad," hardheaded, angry, aggressive, disrespectful, or lazy.

Children are not small adults. Their brains are wired differently and not fully developed. They don't have the same level of wisdom, experience, or problem-solving skills as adults. So it's dangerous when we attribute adult thoughts and reasoning to them. We have to be wise enough to try to understand why children act the way they do by finding out what happened to them and connect the dots between their experiences and behavior.

Discipline and ACEs

Understanding ACEs and toxic stress is so relevant to how we discipline and parent our children. Don't let the way you discipline be a source of ACEs for your child. When you are a parent, it's your job to raise your children peacefully and positively, so your children do not have any trauma.

Children should never experience physical harm, verbal insults, or emotional neglect from their parents, their other caregivers, or any other adult. I've heard parents say there's a difference between spanking and abuse. Well, I say there's a thin line between the two. Spanking—abuse's first cousin—can create a slippery slope causing it to slide right into abuse.

Time out!

Remember, each disciplinary action is not just a "one and done." Each moment adds up and has a lasting impact on our children. The body keeps the score.

So try your very best to do what's best.

Intergenerational Transmission

Children experience adversity most often at the hands of their parents. And the parents were likely traumatized themselves. Trauma is passed down through generations. So what's equally important as an adult is to address your own trauma before handing it off to your kids. We now know that toxic stress from ACEs alters the way genes are expressed, which creates physical, mental, and/or behavioral impairment and is passed to future generations through various biopsychosocial mechanisms. So it's no surprise to see a child with conduct problems who also has a family full of adversity. Therefore, everyone in the family needs help to end the cycle of trauma, build resilience, and promote healing. When we tackle our baggage, we become better humans—better parents, spouses, friends, and coworkers. And most importantly, dealing with your own trauma can stop dysfunction from reaching future generations.

Mechanism by which Adverse Childhood Experiences
Influence Health and Well-being Throughout the Lifespan

Reproduced from Division of Violence Prevention, National Center for Injury Prevention and Control. About the CDC-Kaiser ACE Study. Centers for Disease Control and Prevention. Last reviewed April 6, 2021. Accessed July 30, 2021. https://www.cdc.gov/violenceprevention/aces/about.html.

Prevention

So how do we prevent bad things from happening to our children? Obviously, not all trauma can be prevented. For instance, many children will likely experience a natural disaster or death of a loved one. However, many types of ACEs are preventable and we should be aware of ways to protect our children from them. In addition to preventing ACEs, it's important to prevent toxic stress when ACEs occur. Parents who have the following protective factors are better equipped to prevent adversity and shield their children from toxic stress:

1. Basic Needs

When basic needs, such as food, water, and housing, are met, parents are better able to create a safe, stable, and healthy environment for their family. Certainly, children growing up in poverty feel the weight of adversity and are at risk for toxic stress. They need the support of others to meet basic needs and to reach their fullest potential.

2. Nurturing Environment

Early attachment and a loving and supportive environment are essential for kids to grow, learn, behave, become resilient, and thrive in life. Parents should also consider placing their children in quality, early education settings to stimulate overall learning and should intervene early if delays are identified.

3. Social Support

It truly takes "a village" to raise a child. Parents who have connections with family, with friends, and within the community have more resources to care for their kids. In addition, regular well-child visits with the pediatrician help families prevent, detect, and treat health concerns early.

4. Positive Parenting Skills

Learning how children develop and implementing key parenting strategies help parents manage the daily challenges of parenting, avoid harmful practices, and support healthy development.

5. Social-Emotional Learning

Nurturing and positive relationships within the home and community promote optimal development and behavior in children. It's not all about academics—ABCs, 123s, or reading, writing, and arithmetic. It's also important for a child to be able to express their feelings, regulate their emotions, calm down, handle conflict peacefully, and interact with others by using social norms. Children should learn how to be good and kind humans.

6. Resilience

Some people with ACEs go on to have poor health outcomes as predicted. However, some don't. Want to know what makes the difference? Experts believe it's resilience. The ability to overcome hardship and bounce back from it. If you have this, you're probably doing OK. But if you don't, you may be experiencing some lasting impacts from a dysregulated stress response system that's showing up in your mental health, physical health, behaviors, or combined factors.

We have to build resilience in ourselves and foster it in our children to be able to overcome adversity. Parents who can cope well with the stresses of life often raise children who can do the same. Ann Masten, child development psychologist and researcher in childhood resilience, describes resilience as "ordinary magic." Her work shows that resilience develops in children over time through safe, stable, and nurturing relationships. It is built through play and exposure to ordinary and common daily activities. For example, smiling and talking to your baby during bath time, soothing your upset toddler, reading with your preschooler, building Lego sets with your school-aged child, or talking through a tough decision with your teen all are processes in building resilience. These are positive childhood experiences (PCEs) that protect children in difficult times.

Recent evidence shows that PCEs help counteract the negative impact of ACEs. PCEs promote lifelong health even when children face high doses of ACEs. One study found that the more PCEs a child has, the better their mental health as an adult will be. PCEs are protective and foster connectedness in childhood, leading to an adult who can ask for help and support in difficult times.

There are 7 PCEs that help shape adult mental health.

1. Ability to talk with family about feelings
2. Felt experience that family is supportive in difficult times
3. Enjoyment of participation in community traditions
4. Feeling of belonging in high school
5. Feeling of being supported by friends
6. Having at least 2 nonparent adults who genuinely care
7. Feeling safe and protected by an adult at home

A review of resilience factors to childhood adversity identified 5 modifiable resilience factors that help children cope with and recover from adversity.

1. Individual cognitive traits such as optimism, confidence, and higher executive function skills promote resilience.
2. Responsive parenting and healthy parent-child relationships lessen toxic stress and its effects.

3. Maternal mental health problems increase risk for trauma. Addressing mental health concerns and therapy improve resilience.
4. Self-care skills and healthy routines promote healing (eg, sleep, nutrition, exercise).
5. Understanding trauma influences trauma-focused interventions and better outcomes.

Derived from Traub F, Boynton-Jarrett R. Modifiable resilience factors to childhood adversity for clinical pediatric practice. *Pediatrics.* 2017;139(5):e20162569.

In *Building Resilience in Children and Teens: Giving Kids Roots and Wings,* adolescent medicine specialist Kenneth R. Ginsburg, MD, MS Ed, FAAP, discusses the 7 Cs parents need to build in their kids in order for them to overcome adversity and become successful adults. This book is a must-read for parents.

The 7 Cs: The Essential Building Blocks of Resilience

Bottom Line No. 1: Young people live up or down to expectations we set for them. They need adults who believe in them unconditionally and hold them to the high expectations of being compassionate, generous, and creative.

Competence: When we notice what young people are doing right and give them opportunities to develop important skills, they feel competent. We undermine competence when we don't allow young people to recover themselves after a fall.

Confidence: Young people need confidence to be able to navigate the world, think outside the box, and recover from challenges.

Connection: Connections with other people, schools, and communities offer young people the security that allows them to stand on their own and develop creative solutions.

Character: Young people need a clear sense of right and wrong and a commitment to integrity.

Contribution: Young people who contribute to the well-being of others will receive gratitude rather than condemnation. They will learn that contributing feels good, and they may therefore more easily turn to others, doing so without shame.

Coping: Young people who possess a variety of healthy coping strategies will be less likely to turn to dangerous quick fixes when stressed.

(continued on next page)

Control: Young people who understand that privileges and respect are earned through demonstrated responsibility will learn to make wise choices and will feel a sense of control.

Bottom Line No. 2: What we do to model healthy resilience strategies for our children is more important than anything we say about them.

The 7 Cs are adapted from the Positive Youth Development movement. Rick Little and colleagues at The International Youth Foundation first described the 4 Cs of confidence, competence, connection, and character as the key ingredients needed to ensure a healthy developmental path. They later added contribution because youth with these essential 4 characteristics also contributed to society. The additional 2 Cs—coping and control—allow the model to both promote healthy development and prevent risk.

Resilient individuals likely felt loved, nurtured, and supported by a parent or another caregiver as a child . . . buffers. They had a village, like other family members, friends, teachers, and coaches, who cared about their well-being and who they could go to for help . . . more buffers. They grew up in a safe and stable home environment, with rules and responsibilities. The adults around them believed in them, which boosted their self-confidence and independence . . . and more buffers. They, in turn, believed that anything is possible . . . resilience. The more resilient children are, the more they are able to adapt, overcome, and heal from ACEs and toxic stress.

Screening for ACEs

Screening for ACEs is important to recognize children at risk for toxic stress and poor health outcomes, to prevent toxic stress, and to provide early intervention. The American Academy of Pediatrics recommends that pediatricians routinely screen for ACEs. There are various screening questionnaires. Parents can take the assessment, provide answers for a younger child, or have their teen, 13 years and older, complete it themselves. Schools and other settings should also screen for ACEs, because, unfortunately, some kids don't visit with a doctor regularly.

This is a good spot to screen yourself for ACEs with the following questionnaire:

Pediatric ACEs and Related Life Events Screener (PEARLS)
———— CHILD - To be completed by: **Caregiver** ————

At any point in time since your child was born, has your child seen or been present when the following experiences happened? Please include past and present experiences.

Please note, some questions have more than one part separated by "OR." If any part of the question is answered "Yes," then the answer to the entire question is "Yes."

PART 1:

1. Has your child ever lived with a parent/caregiver who went to jail/prison?

2. Do you think your child ever felt unsupported, unloved and/or unprotected?

3. Has your child ever lived with a parent/caregiver who had mental health issues?
   (for example, depression, schizophrenia, bipolar disorder, PTSD, or an anxiety disorder)

4. Has a parent/caregiver ever insulted, humiliated, or put down your child?

5. Has the child's biological parent or any caregiver ever had, or currently has a problem with too much alcohol, street drugs or prescription medications use?

6. Has your child ever lacked appropriate care by any caregiver?
   (for example, not being protected from unsafe situations, or not cared for when sick or injured even when the resources were available)

7. Has your child ever seen or heard a parent/caregiver being screamed at, sworn at, insulted or humiliated by another adult?

   Or has your child ever seen or heard a parent/caregiver being slapped, kicked, punched beaten up or hurt with a weapon?

8. Has any adult in the household often or very often pushed, grabbed, slapped or thrown something at your child?

   Or has any adult in the household ever hit your child so hard that your child had marks or was injured?

   Or has any adult in the household ever threatened your child or acted in a way that made your child afraid that they might be hurt?

9. Has your child ever experienced sexual abuse?
   (for example, anyone touched your child or asked your child to touch that person in a way that was unwanted, or made your child feel uncomfortable, or anyone ever attempted or actually had oral, anal, or vaginal sex with your child)

10. Have there ever been significant changes in the relationship status of the child's caregiver(s)?
    (for example, a parent/caregiver got a divorce or separated, or a romantic partner moved in or out)

 UCSF Benioff Children's Hospital

Add up the "yes" answers for this first section: [ ]

Please continue to the other side for the rest of questionnaire ——

This tool was created in partnership with UCSF School of Medicine.   Child (Parent/Caregiver Report) – Deidentified

(continued on next page)

PART 2:

1. Has your child ever seen, heard, or been a victim of violence in your neighborhood, community or school?
   (for example, targeted bullying, assault or other violent actions, war or terrorism)

2. Has your child experienced discrimination?
   (for example, being hassled or made to feel inferior or excluded because of their race, ethnicity, gender identity, sexual orientation, religion, learning differences, or disabilities)

3. Has your child ever had problems with housing?
   (for example, being homeless, not having a stable place to live, moved more than two times in a six-month period, faced eviction or foreclosure, or had to live with multiple families or family members)

4. Have you ever worried that your child did not have enough food to eat or that the food for your child would run out before you could buy more?

5. Has your child ever been separated from their parent or caregiver due to foster care, or immigration?

6. Has your child ever lived with a parent/caregiver who had a serious physical illness or disability?

7. Has your child ever lived with a parent or caregiver who died?

Add up the "yes" answers for the second section: ☐

Reproduced from Screening tools. State of California Department of Health Care Services. Accessed June 18, 2021. https://www.acesaware.org/wp-content/uploads/2019/12/PEARLS-Tool-Child-Parent-Caregiver-Report-De-Identified-English.pdf.

You may be shocked by your score just as I was, because we sometimes don't recognize the trauma in our lives. When children experience trauma, it can feel normal, acceptable, and as if it is just a part of life, especially when it happens regularly. The important thing is that you know your score, how that affects your health, and how to start the healing process.

So What Does the Score Mean?

The more ACEs you have, the more at risk you are for poor health outcomes or symptoms of toxic stress.

Each additional ACE increases your risk of developing autoimmune diseases. If you have 4 or more ACEs,

- You're twice as likely to have cardiovascular disease, cancer, or obesity and/or to become a smoker.
- Four times as likely to be depressed.
- Five times as likely to have alcohol use disorder.
- Ten times as likely to develop intravenous drug use.
- Twelve times as likely to attempt suicide.
- Thirty-two times as likely to have learning and behavior problems.

In addition, children who experienced adversity between 9 and 15 years of age were 15% more likely to have severe depression and 25% more likely to have physical health problems, such as asthma and gastrointestinal conditions.

Time out!

Did you know? If you have 6 or more adverse childhood experiences, you're likely to have a 20-year–shorter life span!

Healing and Treating Toxic Stress

ACEs and toxic stress are not the end of the story. Our brains can adapt, and our stress response systems can restore to a steady state. There are hope and ways to beat the toxicity of adversity. Currently, science supports that we can prevent and even reverse the damaging effects of toxic stress.

1. Removing the child from the toxic environment can make all the difference. We must recognize that the child has been traumatized, figure out the type of trauma, and ensure that they aren't retraumatized. For instance, a child who has been physically and emotionally neglected should not be disciplined with time-out. That child already spent much of their life in never-ending time-out, so doing this as a form of discipline would retraumatize them. You must find others ways to correct unwanted behaviors.
2. Having a trauma-informed approach is essential. This approach addresses the "whole" person and considers past trauma and how it influences the individual's behavior when interacting with the individual.

    Specific types of psychotherapy within trauma-informed care are used depending on the nature of the trauma and needs of the person and family.

Specific Types of Psychotherapy

Some of the types of psychotherapy are

► Child-parent psychotherapy (CPP)
► Eye movement desensitization and reprocessing (EMDR)
► Cognitive processing therapy (CPT)
► Prolonged exposure

(continued on next page)

▶ Seeking safety therapy and trauma-focused cognitive behavior therapy (TF-CBT)

To find therapists skilled in trauma, visit www.psychologytoday.com.

Not all children who experience ACEs will need therapy. Recommendation for therapy is based on the type of trauma, your child's ACE score, toxic stress symptoms, or combined factors and will be determined by your child's pediatrician.

Schools should also be a part of the trauma-informed approach.

Trauma-Informed School Resources

▶ "Trauma-Informed Schools" from the Treatment and Services Adaptation Center (https://traumaawareschools.org/traumaInSchools)
▶ "Trauma-Informed Systems: Schools" from The National Child Traumatic Stress Network (NCTSN) (www.nctsn.org/traumainformed-care/creating-trauma-informed-systems/schools)

There are curricula to inform schools on how to recognize trauma and not retraumatize students. Addressing childhood trauma in schools can aid overall academic achievement, reduce disruptive behaviors in the classroom, and improve the social climate of the school. Unfortunately, I don't have enough pages in this book to discuss how the criminal justice system and other institutional sectors in society need a trauma-informed approach as well.

3. When a child has a nurturing and supportive relationship with a caring adult, it can prevent or lessen the damaging effects of toxic stress by stabilizing a dysfunctional stress response system. Ideally, that person should be a parent. However, any caring adult can make a positive impact by sharing and modeling a healthy relationship and promoting PCEs.

4. Lifestyle habits fostering overall health and well-being, such as exercise or play, adequate sleep, and nutrition, help heal the brain and body and improve many of the symptoms of toxic stress. It's equally important for parents to care for themselves in order to provide the best for their kids. Self-care is not selfish! In addition, parenting classes and mindfulness strategies, like meditation, yoga, and deep breathing, are all healing and give parents healthy stress management skills, which promote healing in their children.

ACEs in Practice

Learning about ACES was an aha moment for me (my "her"story). Why hadn't I known about ACEs? I'm a doctor and a lifelong learner! I trained at Johns Hopkins for goodness' sake! But I hadn't learned about them in medical school or residency training. And I'm not that old. I have 4 ACEs, but I am very resilient with way more protective factors and PCEs than ACEs. Still, I do have damage that I'm working to heal.

ACEs also began to inform my thinking about others and the way I managed the behavior of my patients and their families. As I put on my trauma lens, I would question one patient's ADHD diagnosis and the nature of another patient's learning disability. Trauma could explain what was happening in the lives of many of my patients who were having learning, behavior, and medical challenges.

Like Brian and his little sister, Sarah. They were under the care of their maternal grandmother. Their mother was in and out of their lives and currently missing because of a drug addiction. She had been in jail multiple times. Brian, the 10-year-old, had been in the foster care system because of their mom's neglect and drug use. He was having tons of social and behavior issues in school and at home. He was suspended often and got into several fights—one incident caused physical injury. His grandfather disciplined him harshly, with physical and verbal punishment and isolation. You guessed it, he was diagnosed with ADHD, medicated, and receiving behavior therapy that helped a little.

His younger sister was exposed to heroin in the womb. She had developmental delays and was not speaking clearly or behaving like a 5-year-old. She was very hyperactive in the examination room; she responded to instruction by hitting and screaming and didn't adhere to her grandmother's wishes at all. Her grandmother swatted her on the bottom a couple of times, and of course, I discouraged this behavior.

Grandma was so overwhelmed! At the time, I did what I knew to do and recommended developmental and behavioral assessments and therapies for the kids. I also recommended interventions to help at home and at school. I accepted the diagnosis of ADHD in Brian and continued his medication. I knew the circumstances in their lives played into who they were. But I didn't know how much these would affect their health and well-being for a lifetime. Or that there were specific strategies to address their core issue, childhood trauma and toxic stress, not just treat the symptoms.

Now that I know more about trauma, I've spoken with Grandma about ACEs and encouraged her (and Grandad) not to be a source of trauma for the children. I've recommended parenting classes because managing the behavior of those 2 children can't be easy. We've discussed all 5 strategies to reduce the impact of toxic stress in their young lives. Grandma is doing her best, and I already see progress in Brian. He needed a little tender loving care and understanding.

It's funny how things happen, but around this time, an effort was underway to make Central Florida a trauma-informed community. This meant the community as a whole would become ACE aware and consider "What happened to you?" instead of "What's wrong with you?" Somehow, the stars aligned and I was pulled into this effort by some amazing individuals.

We've had well-attended, working conferences, and I've gotten to meet one of the authors of the original Adverse Childhood Experiences Study, Dr Felitti, who was a keynote speaker. I've been energized to raise awareness about ACES, get my colleagues on board, and begin screening my patients.

Currently, I continue to work with the multi-sector group, the Peace and Justice Institute at Valencia College, and speak with various organizations about childhood trauma, symptoms of toxic stress, and healing practices. I follow the American Academy of Pediatrics recommendations and screen for ACES in my patients during well-child visits. I try to help families connect the dots and start the healing process. And I continue to build my resource repertoire and make therapeutic referrals as needed to combat the negative impact of toxic stress. A past president of the American Academy of Pediatrics, Robert Block, MD, FAAP, says, "ACEs are the single greatest unaddressed public health threat facing our nation today." Therefore, every individual, home, and community and the nation should work toward recognizing, preventing, and healing ACEs and toxic stress and building resilience.

Parenting Prescription

Complete the PEARLS questionnaire and screen your kids. Talk with your pediatrician about your score.

PART 5

Establishing a Family Discipline Plan

When this ends, we'll smile sweetly, finally seeing. In testing times, we became the best of beings.

—Amanda Gorman

Chapter 11

Who's Got Skills? You've Got Skills!

Now let's put what you've learned about positive parenting to the test. This chapter is designed for you to examine real-life family situations and decide which pieces of positive parenting and parenting skills are needed to have the most peaceful parent-child interactions. For quick access to all the strategies previously discussed, here are the pieces needed to solve the disciplinary puzzles in this chapter.

Essential Discipline Dynamics (Part 2), Child Basics: Act Like a Parent but Think Like a Child (Part 4)

1. Knowledge of Child Development and Parenting Skills

- Early Childhood, or the Critical Years: Birth to 3 Years (Chapter 6)
- Preschool Period: 3 to 5 Years (Chapter 7), including life skills (eg, sharing) and conflict resolution for preschoolers
- School-age Period: 6 to 12 Years (Chapter 8), including emotion coaching, other anger management tips, and helping siblings get along better (eg, quality time for each child)
- Adolescence: 12 to 17 Years (Chapter 9), including keeping it real and peer pressure and toxic relationships
- Be Aware: From ACEs to Healing (Chapter 10), including resilience

2. Good Relational Health Between Parent and Child

- Love and affection
- Honesty
- Respect
- Connection (eg, empathy)
- Belonging

- Support
- A friendly relationship

3. Encouraging Positive Behavior

- Positive reinforcement (eg, rewards, praise)
- Negative reinforcement
- Positive instructions

4. Discouraging and Correcting Negative Behavior

- Coaching cues, including verbal prompts (eg, countdown) and nonverbal prompts (nurturing but firm voice)
- Consequences (eg, natural or logical)
- First, picking your battles
- Attention (eg, removing attention)
- Redirection and distraction

5. Managing the Environment

- Being proactive, not reactive (eg, getting creative)
- Establishing structure and routines
- Setting limits and rules
- Giving choices

Adult in the Mirror (Part 3)

- "Selfie" skills (Chapter 3)
  — Self-reflection
  — Self-care
- Top model skills (Chapter 4)
- Woosah skills (Chapter 5)
  — Mindfulness
  — Coping skills
  — Growth mindset

Scenario 1. Lack of Knowledge

A 6-month-old baby and her father are visiting the doctor for a well-child checkup. The doctor overhears the father talking on speakerphone and he occasionally yells at his baby to be quiet and to stop kicking. He sounds angry and irritated.

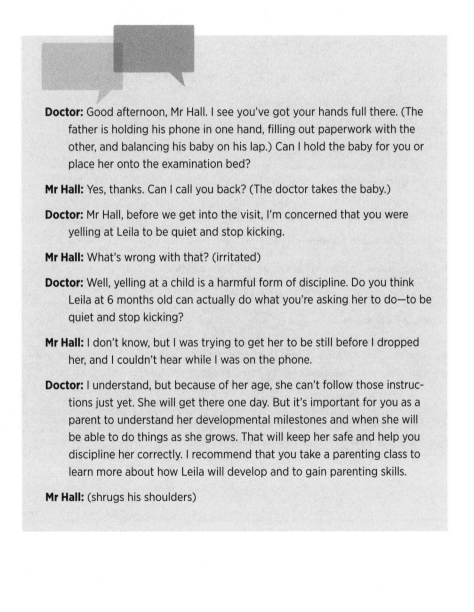

Doctor: Good afternoon, Mr Hall. I see you've got your hands full there. (The father is holding his phone in one hand, filling out paperwork with the other, and balancing his baby on his lap.) Can I hold the baby for you or place her onto the examination bed?

Mr Hall: Yes, thanks. Can I call you back? (The doctor takes the baby.)

Doctor: Mr Hall, before we get into the visit, I'm concerned that you were yelling at Leila to be quiet and stop kicking.

Mr Hall: What's wrong with that? (irritated)

Doctor: Well, yelling at a child is a harmful form of discipline. Do you think Leila at 6 months old can actually do what you're asking her to do—to be quiet and stop kicking?

Mr Hall: I don't know, but I was trying to get her to be still before I dropped her, and I couldn't hear while I was on the phone.

Doctor: I understand, but because of her age, she can't follow those instructions just yet. She will get there one day. But it's important for you as a parent to understand her developmental milestones and when she will be able to do things as she grows. That will keep her safe and help you discipline her correctly. I recommend that you take a parenting class to learn more about how Leila will develop and to gain parenting skills.

Mr Hall: (shrugs his shoulders)

Test Time!

1. What did Mr Hall do well in this scenario?

2. How can Mr Hall improve in this scenario?

3. Which one of the following High Five Essentials is critical for this interaction?

    a. Encouraging Positive Behavior

    b. Knowledge of Child Development and Parenting Skills

    c. Managing the Environment

    d. Discouraging and Correcting Negative Behavior

4. This situation could have been prevented if Mr Hall

    a. Hadn't used his phone during the visit

    b. Secured his baby in her carrier or on the examination bed

    c. Had realistic expectations of his child

    d. All the above

5. True or false: If Mr Hall agrees to go to parenting class, there is no need for the pediatrician to investigate Leila's home environment for protective factors.

Scenario Skills: Knowledge of Child Development and Parenting Skills, Managing the Environment, woosah skills, child basics (safety)

Scenario 2. Who's Bullying Who?

William is a 10-year-old boy, and his school principal is calling his dad, Mr Jacobs.

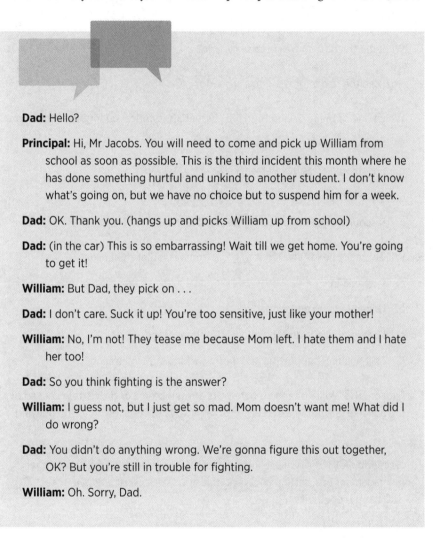

Dad: Hello?

Principal: Hi, Mr Jacobs. You will need to come and pick up William from school as soon as possible. This is the third incident this month where he has done something hurtful and unkind to another student. I don't know what's going on, but we have no choice but to suspend him for a week.

Dad: OK. Thank you. (hangs up and picks William up from school)

Dad: (in the car) This is so embarrassing! Wait till we get home. You're going to get it!

William: But Dad, they pick on . . .

Dad: I don't care. Suck it up! You're too sensitive, just like your mother!

William: No, I'm not! They tease me because Mom left. I hate them and I hate her too!

Dad: So you think fighting is the answer?

William: I guess not, but I just get so mad. Mom doesn't want me! What did I do wrong?

Dad: You didn't do anything wrong. We're gonna figure this out together, OK? But you're still in trouble for fighting.

William: Oh. Sorry, Dad.

Test Time!

1. What did the dad do well in this scenario?

2. How can the dad improve in this scenario?

3. Which one of the following High Five Essentials is critical during this interaction?

    a. Managing the Environment

    b. Encouraging Positive Behavior

    c. Good Relational Health Between Parent and Child

    d. Discouraging and Correcting Negative Behavior

5. William really needs all except _____ from his father right now.

    a. A spanking

    b. Understanding and empathy

    c. Loss of privilege and to write a letter of apology

    d. Skill building/support (ie, emotion coaching and counseling)

5. True or false: William's recent behaviors are symptoms of toxic stress caused by the adverse childhood experiences of family dysfunction, divorce, and bullying.

Scenario Skills: resilience, connection, empathy, consequences, other anger management tips, setting limits and rules (includes expectations), woosah skills, top model skills

Scenario 3. "Bad Kid" or Just Misunderstood?

A 6-year-old-boy is at home with his mom. He is jumping on and off his bed and throwing toys and play fighting. His room is a mess. He zips by his mom while she is on the phone.

Mom: (on phone with dad) Please hurry up and get home. I need a break!

Dad: On my way. What's going on?

Mom: The usual—our wild and crazy kid. He never sits still. He's so messy and refuses to clean up. He only wants to watch TV and play electronics all day. He doesn't pay attention or remember anything when we do schoolwork. Then he refuses and goes berserk. I just don't know what to do.

Dad: We've tried it your way. Now it's time to go "old school." No more being nice, talking, and time-outs. I'm tired of the school calling and the disrespect and disobedience.

Mom: Wait, let's talk about this. You know I was abused as a child, and I don't want that for Ryan. But I am about to lose it. Maybe he just needs more time to grow up, or maybe we should talk with the pediatrician like the school suggested. We need help.

Test Time!

1. What did the Mom do well in this scenario?

2. How can the parents improve in this scenario?

3. Which 2 of the following High Five Essentials are critical for this interaction?

    a. Knowledge of Child Development and Parenting Skills

    b. Good Relational Health Between Parent and Child

    c. Managing the Environment

    d. Discouraging and Correcting Negative Behavior

4. Ryan really needs all except _____ from his parents right now.

    a. Medication

    b. Understanding and empathy

    c. Behavioral, developmental, and educational evaluation

    d. Positive reinforcement and structure and routines

5. True or false: Ryan is just a kid behaving badly who needs more strict parenting.

Scenario Skills: support (evaluation and therapy), asking the pediatrician, Knowledge of Child Development and Parenting Skills, top model skills, emotion coaching, time-out, verbal prompts, countdown, establishing structure and routines, praise, rewards, consequences, negative reinforcement, mindfulness, self-care, knowing when to ask for help

Scenario 4. Can Y'all Just Get Along?

Siblings Bella (8 years of age), Paige (5 years), and Cesily (3 years) are at home with their mom. They are currently pushing and fighting over the remote control and yelling at each other loudly. Mom is multitasking, working on the computer and cooking dinner, while being interrupted by the girls' complaining constantly.

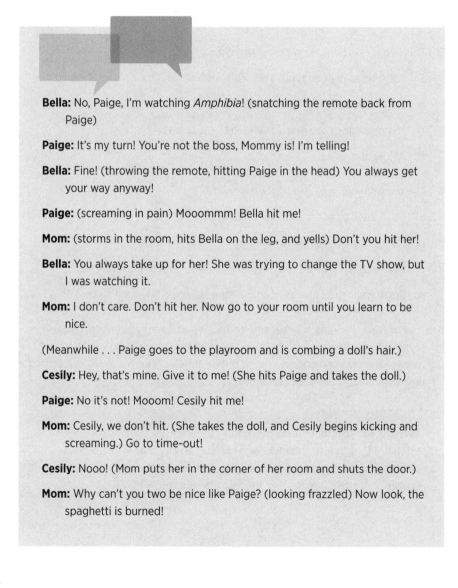

Bella: No, Paige, I'm watching *Amphibia*! (snatching the remote back from Paige)

Paige: It's my turn! You're not the boss, Mommy is! I'm telling!

Bella: Fine! (throwing the remote, hitting Paige in the head) You always get your way anyway!

Paige: (screaming in pain) Mooommm! Bella hit me!

Mom: (storms in the room, hits Bella on the leg, and yells) Don't you hit her!

Bella: You always take up for her! She was trying to change the TV show, but I was watching it.

Mom: I don't care. Don't hit her. Now go to your room until you learn to be nice.

(Meanwhile . . . Paige goes to the playroom and is combing a doll's hair.)

Cesily: Hey, that's mine. Give it to me! (She hits Paige and takes the doll.)

Paige: No it's not! Mooom! Cesily hit me!

Mom: Cesily, we don't hit. (She takes the doll, and Cesily begins kicking and screaming.) Go to time-out!

Cesily: Nooo! (Mom puts her in the corner of her room and shuts the door.)

Mom: Why can't you two be nice like Paige? (looking frazzled) Now look, the spaghetti is burned!

Test Time!

1. What did the mom do well in this scenario?

2. How can the mom improve in this scenario?

3. This family is experiencing sibling rivalry because

    a. The girls have poor conflict resolution skills.

    b. Bella is jealous of her younger sibling.

    c. The mom gives too much attention to the drama.

    d. All the above.

4. The mom should _____ to lessen the rivalry.

    a. Send them all to their rooms as punishment.

    b. Shame them for not getting along.

    c. Buy each girl a TV and separate toys so they won't fight over them.

    d. Create private space for "me time" and schedule "Mommy and me time."

5. True or false: The girls may become aggressive when they get upset because their mom models the same behavior. Instead, the mom should keep her cool, manage the environment, and spend quality time with each child to demonstrate how to interact nicely with one another.

Scenario Skills: attention, nurturing but firm voice, positive instructions, establishing structure and routines, time-out, quality time for each child (eg, playtime), Encouraging Positive Behavior, consequences, sharing, conflict resolution for preschoolers, top model skills, woosah skills

Scenario 5. The "P" Word

Brandon is a 14-year-old going through puberty who wants more privacy. He's been rebellious, moody, and disrespectful.

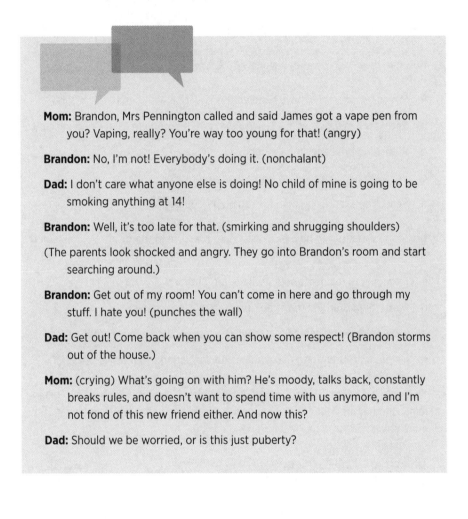

Mom: Brandon, Mrs Pennington called and said James got a vape pen from you? Vaping, really? You're way too young for that! (angry)

Brandon: No, I'm not! Everybody's doing it. (nonchalant)

Dad: I don't care what anyone else is doing! No child of mine is going to be smoking anything at 14!

Brandon: Well, it's too late for that. (smirking and shrugging shoulders)

(The parents look shocked and angry. They go into Brandon's room and start searching around.)

Brandon: Get out of my room! You can't come in here and go through my stuff. I hate you! (punches the wall)

Dad: Get out! Come back when you can show some respect! (Brandon storms out of the house.)

Mom: (crying) What's going on with him? He's moody, talks back, constantly breaks rules, and doesn't want to spend time with us anymore, and I'm not fond of this new friend either. And now this?

Dad: Should we be worried, or is this just puberty?

Test Time!

1. What did the parents do well in this scenario?

2. How can they improve in this scenario?

3. Brandon's parents could have handled this situation with him better by first

    a. Sitting down together and talking through the problem calmly and peacefully

    b. Removing privileges for a month

    c. Enrolling him in a tobacco prevention program

    d. Searching Brandon's room for vaping paraphernalia

4. Brandon's parents can help him resist peer pressure in the future by doing all the following things except

    a. Engaging in real talk about teenage temptations

    b. Forbidding Brandon from vaping ever again

    c. Helping Brandon come up with ways to say no but keep his "cool points"

    d. Listening to Brandon's perspective and correcting misinformation

5. True or false: Brandon's parents should take him to see his pediatrician to determine whether his behavioral changes are consistent with puberty or something more concerning and for teen parenting advice.

Scenario Skills: Knowledge of Child Development and Parenting Skills, Good Relational Health Between Parent and Child, consequences, woosah skills, keeping it real, peer pressure and toxic relationships, setting limits and rules, empathy

Scenario 6. Am I Grown Yet?

Jennifer is a 17-year-old girl visiting the doctor's office for a depression screening with her mom, Ms Young. Jennifer's mom is stressed.

Doctor: Ms Young, Jennifer's screening for depression was concerning. I spoke with her privately and confirmed that she has a lot of stressors. Do you think we could find some ways to help her cope better?

Ms Young: We both need help with coping better. I struggle with depression. I lost my job during the pandemic, we can barely make ends meet, and she hasn't adjusted well to virtual school and being away from her friends. We're arguing all the time, because she doesn't do anything I ask or help around the house, stays in her room on the phone all night, and wants to sleep all day.

Doctor: I'm sorry you're going through these difficult times. I would like to refer you both to our social worker and counselor to help with resources and manage all of this stress. Let's talk with Jennifer about some changes I think you both should make at home.

Ms Young: OK.

Doctor: Jennifer, your mom was explaining how things have been at home lately. We thought it might be good to give you some responsibilities around the house and ask that you also make some changes that would help you feel better. Ms Young, what do you need from Jennifer?

Ms Young: Jenn, we're both going to talk with someone to help us feel better. I need your help around the house, and that includes your room. I'm going to take your phone at bedtime so you can get some sleep, which will help you feel better and do better in school. And I hope we can push each other to get out of the house more and get some exercise.

Jennifer: You're not taking my phone! I go to bed when I'm sleepy. And your room's a mess too!

(continued on next page)

Doctor: Jennifer, you're not an adult yet. Even though you want to do things in your way, your mom and I are helping you choose what's best for you, because we care. You both are going through a lot right now. What are you willing to do to help? Is there something your mom can do for you if you can do what she asks?

Jennifer: Weeelll, I want to see my friends more and maybe get a job this summer to have my own money.

Ms Young: Deal! Get your grades up, clean up after yourself, and go to sleep at night, and we can work on those goals.

Jennifer: OK. (reluctantly)

Doctor: Shake on it? (Jennifer and her Mom happily shake hands.)

Test Time!

1. What did Ms Young do well in this scenario?

2. How can she improve in this scenario?

3. Jennifer is facing many adversities. Ms Young can help her build resilience by

    a. Strengthening their parent-teen relationship

    b. Naming 3 things they are thankful for, daily

    c. Improving parenting strategies

    d. All the above

4. Both Ms Young and Jennifer should use all the following coping skills to manage their stress except

    a. Positive self-talk.

    b. Plan your day—schoolwork, exercise, cleaning, and free time.

    c. Overindulgence—oversleeping, overeating, or excessive screen time.

    d. Ask for help.

5. True or false: Jennifer is more likely to obey Ms Young if Jennifer is offered an explanation for rules, given choices, feels heard, and is able to gain more independence.

Scenario Skills: Knowledge of Child Development and Parenting Skills, Good Relational Health Between Parent and Child, coping skills, awareness of adverse childhood experiences, resilience, self-care, top model skills

Answer Guide

Scenario 1. Lack of Knowledge

Question 1. What did Mr Hall do well in this scenario?

Answer: Mr Hall brought his child to the pediatrician for her well-child visit. While talking on his phone, he was trying his best to balance his baby on his lap.

Question 2. How can Mr Hall improve in this scenario?

Answer: Mr Hall can be better in this scenario by holding onto his baby and not trying to multitask at the same time. Instead of telling his child to stop kicking and to be quiet, he can try to entertain her to keep her busy. At 6 months old, she is developmentally too young to understand those requests.

Question 3.

Answer: B

Question 4.

Answer: D

Question 5.

Answer: False

Scenario 2. Who's Bullying Who

Question 1. What did the dad do well in this scenario?

Answer: The dad listened to his son and was supportive when he heard his son share his feelings. The dad explained to his son that he can't fight and there were consequences.

Question 2. How can the dad improve in this scenario?

Answer: The dad can keep his cool, model self-control, and not call names or label or threaten about the future.

Question 3.

Answer: C

Question 4.

Answer: A

Question 5.

Answer: True

Scenario 3. "Bad Kid" or Just Misunderstood?

Question 1. What did the mom do well in this scenario?

Answer: The mom realized that her son's actions were causing her to feel really upset, and she called her husband and told him she needed a break. She communicated her concerns to her husband and refused to use negative discipline. She wanted to reach out and get help for the situation.

Question 2. How can the parents improve in this scenario?

Answer: The parents can woosah (relax) and practice self-care. They can't give up on their son or label him. The dad can't go "old school" on him. By reaching out to a counselor or their pediatrician, maybe they can provide help and determine whether there might be a medical problem or behavior issue.

Question 3.

Answer: A and C

Question 4:

Answer: A

Question 5:

Answer: False

Scenario 4. Can Y'all Just Get Along?

Question 1. What did the Mom do well in this scenario?

Answer: She did the best she could to multitask. She was trying to discipline by using consequences.

Question 2. How can the mom improve in this scenario?

Answer: She can woosah (relax) and take a breath. She can model positive behavior by teaching her daughters to be fair and to stop hitting. She can use the time-out correctly and realize that Paige never went to her room for her time-out. She can give a consequence for that misbehavior. She can avoid verbally comparing her kids.

Question 3.

Answer: D

Question 4.

Answer: D

Question 5.

Answer: True

Scenario 5. The "P" Word

Question 1. What did the parents do well in this scenario?

Answer: The parents showed genuine concern and checked their son's bedroom for drugs and vaping pens. They explained to him that they have expectations that need to be followed.

Question 2. How can they improve in this scenario?

Answer: First woosah (relax) and take a breath. Take the time you need to relax, and think about what you want to say first. Explain the dangers of vaping to your teen so he really understands, instead of just saying don't do it and yelling. Be specific about what the consequences will be if your teen does it again.

Question 3.

Answer: A

Question 4.

Answer: B

Question 5.

Answer: True

Scenario 6. Am I Grown Yet?

Question 1. What did Ms Young do well in this scenario?

Answer: Ms Young was open and honest with the doctor. She accepted her help, and together, they created an action plan.

Question 2. How can she improve in this scenario?

Answer: Ms Young can try to set a better example for her daughter by cleaning her own room and then helping her daughter clean hers. She can follow through with getting some counseling for both of them. She can continue to teach Jennifer about being responsible and independent. And she can encourage them both to get out and get some exercise, which will improve both of their stress levels.

Question 3.

Answer: D

Question 4.

Answer: C

Question 5.

Answer: True

Chapter 12

Piecing Together a Plan

Imagine yourself becoming that "boss" mom or dad or other caregiver who knows how to maneuver your kids through any situation. You know, the one from the beginning of this book who skillfully uses positive parenting to raise happy, healthy, well-behaved kids. Well, you're on your way and so are your kids. So put a smile on your face, and give each other a celebratory high five!

One day, in the not so distant future, you will be a grandparent watching your adult child playing with your grandkids, all the while reminiscing on their childhood with all its challenges and successes. You will realize it was all a process, not any one moment (good or bad) but everything you did, to help get them to where they are right now—a productive, kind, successful parent, wife/husband, professional, and human. You will realize you did it and breathe a sigh of relief. Job well done!

As a pediatrician and mother of 2 children, I've lived much of what I've written. I wrote this book with the goal of helping your family with a positive parenting plan. Please know that I'm working right alongside you to be the best parent I can be. My goal is also to raise happy, healthy, well-behaved kids who are successful and productive in society.

Now that you understand the importance of the High Five Essentials, I encourage you to sit down with your family and begin to piece together a family discipline plan. After all, that's the whole point of this book—to come up with a plan to discipline your kids peacefully, positively, and effectively. Once you create a plan, it will change over time as your child grows and develops, or you may need to tweak things you identify that don't seem to work for your child. And by all means, share your plan with teachers, babysitters, and other family members so you all are working together on the same plan and offering the same messages.

To support your efforts, here is an example plan, the Hall Family Discipline Plan.

The _____Hall Family_____ Discipline Plan

Behavior Concerns

_____Jonathan Hall_____ , _____11 years old_____
Child Name   Age

Child

Summarize the behavior concerns you have about your child.

Jonathan is having homework struggles and often forgets to complete his chores. He has difficulty taking responsibility for poor choices. When I discipline him with consequences, he sometimes yells and talks back to me. He breaks the rules by playing video games excessively. He and his little sister constantly argue.

Parent

Summarize the behavior concerns you have about your parenting style. (Part 3)

As a parent, I find myself getting angry when my son repeatedly fails to follow instructions and complete chores. I find myself yelling at my son when he talks back to me. I become very frustrated when he gets emotional during homework. I'm inconsistent with giving consequences and, instead, default to yelling and sometimes hitting when I've had enough. I'm always threatening consequences when my kids argue, and I feel stuck with policing the conflict.

Building Better Behaviors by Using the High Five Essentials (Part 2)

1. Knowledge of Child Development and Parenting Skills (Chapter 2)

Summarize the age-specific, developmental knowledge and parenting skills that you will use for this child.

As a parent, I understand that my son, Jonathan, who is a middle schooler, has some body and mood changes of early puberty. He craves independence and values time with his friends, which he has less of during the COVID-19 pandemic. He lacks confidence and focus/

attention in school. I think he may have attention-deficit/hyperactivity disorder (ADHD). He feels angry and yells back when he is yelled at. I realize that he lies to get out of trouble and speaks before he thinks. He complains that his little sister is always in his things and gets him into trouble.

I now have a better understanding of what goes on during Jonathan's middle school developmental stage, which helps me form realistic expectations for him. I realize that he faces challenges just as I do, especially during the pandemic. I will allow some earned independence and privacy but supervise from a distance. I will talk with his pediatrician about my concerns of ADHD and will get creative with ways he can safely spend time with his friends. I will identify positive strategies to address his anger, lying, not following the rules, and sibling conflict. And I will carve out some quality time just for him.

What additional age-specific, developmental knowledge and parenting skills can you use for this child? Check off each one that applies.

Baby (Chapter 6)
- ☐ Bonding and attachment
- ☐ Nurturing
- ☐ Responding
- ☐ Early learning and play
- ☐ Other

Toddler (Chapter 6)
- ☐ Patience and understanding
- ☐ Fostering independence
- ☐ Early detection and early intervention
- ☐ Acknowledging their emotions
- ☐ Helping them use their words

(continued on next page)

☐ Calling time-out

☐ Asking a question: "Is that a good choice?"

☐ Redirection

☐ Distraction

☐ Countdown

☐ Positive reinforcement

☐ Giving choices

☐ Other

Preschooler (Chapter 7)

☐ "Ask me anything" time

☐ Replying with the same or a similar question so your child can answer it for themselves

☐ Teaching life skills (eg, sharing)

☐ Ensuring school readiness (eg, literacy)

☐ Encouraging self-help skills (eg, putting on clothes)

☐ Co-regulation

☐ Promoting conflict resolution

☐ Problem-solving

☐ Nonadherence bag of tricks (eg, leverage your loving relationship, count down, give a choice, call a time-out)

☐ Other

Child (Chapter 8)

☐ Allowing some independence

☐ Parenting from a distance

☑ Check-in

☑ Emotion coaching and other anger management tips (eg, avoid triggers, prompt calming skills)

☑ Helping siblings get along better (eg, set aside quality time for each child, don't compare your kids, role-play conflict resolution)

☐ Handling lying (eg, redirect, ask a clarifying question, give a chance, praise honesty, give consequences)

☐ Other

Teen (Chapter 9)

☐ Keeping it real

☐ "Seeing" them

☐ Stimulating adult practice (eg, money management, employment)

☐ Providing a stepwise approach to independence and allowing privacy within limits

☐ Staying current and speaking your teen's language

☐ Guiding your teen through peer pressure as needed

☐ Dating preparation

☐ Other

If Trauma Is an Issue (Chapter 10)

☐ Trauma-informed care

☐ Providing safe, stable, nurturing relationships and environments

☐ Promoting positive childhood experiences

☐ Positive parenting skills

☐ Having social support

☐ Promoting social-emotional learning

☐ Healing practices (eg, proper nutrition, sleep, or exercise; mindfulness)

☐ Building resilience

☐ Trauma-focused therapy

☐ Other

2. Good Relational Health Between Parent and Child (Chapter 2)

Summarize the parental relational skills that you will use for this child.

As a parent, I will focus on strengthening our relationship to build unconditional love, trust, and respect. Jonathan's love languages are Quality Time and Words of Affirmation. I will set aside time each day to check in with him and praise him when he makes good choices, show him respect by trying not to yell at him or hit him, be honest about my frustrations and allow him to do the same, provide academic support calmly or find someone who can, and create a sense of belonging by including him in family responsibilities, decisions, and activities.

What parental relational skills can you use for this child? Check off each one that applies.

- ☑ Love and affection
- ☑ Connection (eg, empathy, listening)
- ☐ Belonging
- ☐ Trust
- ☑ Mutual respect
- ☐ Acceptance
- ☐ Honesty
- ☐ Support
- ☑ A friendly relationship
- ☐ Providing a stepwise approach to independence
- ☐ Other

3. Encouraging Positive Behavior (Chapter 2)

Summarize the parenting skills that you will use for this child to encourage wanted or desired behavior.

As a parent, I will teach Jonathan how to behave by showing him what to do, giving positive instructions, paying attention to what I want to see, and using reinforcement strategies. I will "catch him being good" more than I address misbehavior and set up a reward chart and incentives regarding his chores, homework, screen time, and interactions with his little sister.

What parenting skills can you use for this child to encourage wanted or desired behavior? Check off each one that applies.

- ☑ Modeling proper behavior
- ☑ Attention (giving attention to wanted behaviors)
- ☑ Positive reinforcement (eg, praise, rewards, incentives)
- ☐ Negative reinforcement ("Until you do this . . . you can't do that")
- ☑ Positive instructions (in a singsong voice, like "Clean up what you mess up" vs "Don't be messy")
- ☐ Other

4. Discouraging and Correcting Negative Behavior (Chapter 2)

Summarize the parenting skills for inappropriate behavior that you will use for this child.

As Jonathan's parent, I will hold him accountable for poor choices by setting expectations and applying consequences consistently when he fails to uphold rules and routines. I will redirect him with various prompts when he is off task. If the misbehavior is not a big deal or not a "deal breaker," I will not intervene and I will let natural consequences prevail. I will look for teachable moments in songs, movies, personal stories, and everyday life. I will speak in a nurturing but firm voice to correct Jonathan when he misbehaves. I will use emotion coaching to co-regulate with him when emotions get out of hand.

What parenting skills for inappropriate behavior can you use for this child? Check off each one that applies.

- ☑ First, picking your battles (correcting "deal breaker" behaviors)
- ☑ Attention (eg, removing attention from unwanted behaviors)
- ☐ Redirection and distraction
- ☑ Coaching cues (verbal [eg, countdown] or nonverbal prompts)
- ☐ Telling a story, singing a song
- ☑ Consequences (eg, natural or logical; time-out balanced with "time in")
- ☐ Other

---

5. Managing the Environment (Chapter 2)

Summarize the environment-related parenting skills that you will use for this child.

I realize now that I cannot control Jonathan (doing so undermines our relational health), but I can control the environment to improve his behavior and help him make good choices. I will make morning and bedtime routine checklists, make sure we get things ready the night before to lessen stress, and make and review house rules with Jonathan. He will repeat the rules and discuss consequences for nonadherence. I will do my best to offer him choices to promote independence, confidence, problem-solving skills, and appropriate decision-making.

What environment-related parenting skills can you use for this child? Check off each one that applies.

- ☐ Being proactive, not reactive (planning, anticipating, or getting creative)
- ☑ Establishing structure and routines
- ☑ Setting limits and rules (eg, minimize temptations, give choices)
- ☐ Other

Building Better Behaviors by Focusing on the Adult in the Mirror (Part 3)

"Selfie" Skills (Chapter 3)

Summarize the selfie skills that you will use to interact better with this child.

I don't want to yell at my kids, put them down, or hit them. I will work on showing them the love and respect we all deserve. To manage stress, I will get adequate sleep, schedule "me time," and exercise to replenish myself.

What "selfie" skills do I need to work on? Check off each one that applies.

- ☐ Mirror checks
- ☑ Being a "grow" parent
- ☑ Self-care plan
- ☑ Emotional intelligence
- ☐ Other

Top Model Skills (Chapter 4)

Summarize the top model skills that you will use to interact better with this child.

If I yell, hit, and show disrespect, my kids will too. I will use my new-found parenting skills to respond to my kids appropriately when they misbehave. I will also try to focus on their strengths and good choices.

What top model skills do I need to work on? Check off each one that applies.

- ☐ Self-improvement
- ☑ Self-control
- ☐ Fairness
- ☐ Honesty
- ☑ Kindness
- ☑ Optimism
- ☐ Responsibility
- ☐ Other

Woosah Skills (Chapter 5)

Summarize the woosah skills that you will use to interact better with this child.

I will take a deep breath and count to 10 before I respond to my kids when I feel frustrated or angry. I would like to pray, meditate, and name 3 things I am grateful for each morning and at bedtime.

What woosah skills do I need to work on ? Check off each one that applies.

- ☑ Mindfulness (eg, deep breathing, meditation, yoga)
- ☑ Mindful parenting
- ☑ Positive coping skills
- ☐ Growth mindset
- ☐ Other

Now it's your turn! Below is a blank family discipline plan for your own family's use. This template can be printed from my website (www.drcandicemd.com).

The _____ Discipline Plan

Behavior Concerns

_____ , _____
                     Child Name   Age

Child

Summarize the behavior concerns you have about your child.

_____

_____

_____

_____

_____

Parent

Summarize the behavior concerns you have about your parenting style. (Part 3)

_____

_____

_____

_____

_____

Building Better Behaviors by Using the High Five Essentials (Part 2)

1. Knowledge of Child Development and Parenting Skills (Chapter 2)

Summarize the age-specific, developmental knowledge and parenting skills that you will use for this child.

_____

_____

_____

_____

_____

_____

What additional age-specific, developmental knowledge and parenting skills can you use for this child? Check off each one that applies.

Baby (Chapter 6)

☐ Bonding and attachment

☐ Nurturing

☐ Responding

☐ Early learning and play

☐ Other

Toddler (Chapter 6)

☐ Patience and understanding

☐ Fostering independence

☐ Early detection and early intervention

☐ Acknowledging their emotions

☐ Helping them use their words

☐ Calling time-out

☐ Asking a question: "Is that a good choice?"

☐ Redirection

☐ Distraction

☐ Countdown

(continued on next page)

☐ Positive reinforcement

☐ Giving choices

☐ Other

Preschooler (Chapter 7)

☐ "Ask me anything" time

☐ Replying with the same or a similar question so your child can answer it for themselves

☐ Teaching life skills (eg, sharing)

☐ Ensuring school readiness (eg, literacy)

☐ Encouraging self-help skills (eg, putting on clothes)

☐ Co-regulation

☐ Promoting conflict resolution

☐ Problem-solving

☐ Nonadherence bag of tricks (eg, leverage your loving relationship, count down, give a choice, call a time-out)

☐ Other

Child (Chapter 8)

☐ Allowing some independence

☐ Parenting from a distance

☐ Check-in

☐ Emotion coaching and other anger management tips (eg, avoid triggers, prompt calming skills)

☐ Helping siblings get along better (eg, set aside quality time for each child, don't compare your kids, role-play conflict resolution)

☐ Handling lying (eg, redirect, ask a clarifying question, give a chance, praise honesty, give consequences)

☐ Other

Teen (Chapter 9)

☐ Keeping it real

☐ "Seeing" them

☐ Stimulating adult practice (eg, money management, employment)

☐ Providing a stepwise approach to independence and allowing privacy within limits

☐ Staying current and speaking your teen's language

☐ Guiding your teen through peer pressure as needed

☐ Dating preparation

☐ Other

If Trauma Is an Issue (Chapter 10)

☐ Trauma-informed care

☐ Providing safe, stable, nurturing relationships and environments

☐ Promoting positive childhood experiences

☐ Positive parenting skills

☐ Having social support

☐ Promoting social-emotional learning

☐ Healing practices (eg, proper nutrition, sleep, or exercise; mindfulness)

☐ Building resilience

☐ Trauma-focused therapy

☐ Other

2. Good Relational Health Between Parent and Child (Chapter 2)

Summarize the parental relational skills that you will use for this child.

_____

_____

_____

_____

_____

_____

What parental relational skills can you use for this child? Check off each one that applies.

☐ Love and affection

☐ Connection (eg, empathy, listening)

☐ Belonging

☐ Trust

(continued on next page)

☐ Mutual respect

☐ Acceptance

☐ Honesty

☐ Support

☐ A friendly relationship

☐ Providing a stepwise approach to independence

☐ Other

3. Encouraging Positive Behavior (Chapter 2)

Summarize the parenting skills that you will use for this child to encourage wanted or desired behavior.

_____

_____

_____

_____

_____

_____

What parenting skills can you use for this child to encourage wanted or desired behavior? Check off each one that applies.

☐ Modeling proper behavior

☐ Attention (giving attention to wanted behaviors)

☐ Positive reinforcement (eg, praise, rewards, incentives)

☐ Negative reinforcement ("Until you do this . . . you can't do that")

☐ Positive instructions (in a singsong voice, like "Clean up what you mess up" vs "Don't be messy")

☐ Other

4. Discouraging and Correcting Negative Behavior (Chapter 2)

Summarize the parenting skills for inappropriate behavior that you will use for this child.

_____

_____

_____

_____

_____

_____

What parenting skills for inappropriate behavior can you use for this child? Check off each one that applies.

☐ First, picking your battles (correcting "deal breaker" behaviors)

☐ Attention (eg, removing attention from unwanted behaviors)

☐ Redirection and distraction

☐ Coaching cues (verbal [eg, countdown] or nonverbal prompts)

☐ Telling a story, singing a song

☐ Consequences (eg, natural or logical; time-out balanced with "time in")

☐ Other

5. Managing the Environment (Chapter 2)

Summarize the environment-related parenting skills that you will use for this child.

_____

_____

_____

_____

_____

_____

What environment-related parenting skills can you use for this child? Check off each one that applies.

☐ Being proactive, not reactive (planning, anticipating, or getting creative)

☐ Establishing structure and routines

☐ Setting limits and rules (eg, minimize temptations, give choices)

☐ Other

Building Better Behaviors by Focusing on the Adult in the Mirror (Part 3)

"Selfie" Skills (Chapter 3)

Summarize the selfie skills that you will use to interact better with this child.

_____

_____

_____

_____

_____

_____

What "selfie" skills do I need to work on? Check off each one that applies.

☐ Mirror checks

☐ Being a "grow" parent

☐ Self-care plan

☐ Emotional intelligence

☐ Other

Top Model Skills (Chapter 4)

Summarize the top model skills that you will use to interact better with this child.

_____

_____

_____

_____

_____

_____

What top model skills do I need to work on? Check off each one that applies.

- ☐ Self-improvement
- ☐ Self-control
- ☐ Fairness
- ☐ Honesty
- ☐ Kindness
- ☐ Optimism
- ☐ Responsibility
- ☐ Other

Woosah Skills (Chapter 5)

Summarize the woosah skills that you will use to interact better with this child.

_____

_____

_____

_____

_____

_____

What woosah skills do I need to work on? Check off each one that applies.

- ☐ Mindfulness (eg, deep breathing, meditation, yoga)
- ☐ Mindful parenting
- ☐ Positive coping skills
- ☐ Growth mindset
- ☐ Other

This book is overflowing with parenting and discipline guidance. It's a plan, and everyone needs to work together to be successful. Please remember these take-home messages.

Discipline is all about teaching and guiding your child. You are the teacher. Your child is the student. You never have to harm your child when disciplining them. Spanking, threatening, controlling, and demeaning are all negative forms of discipline that hurt kids and have potential long-term negative outcomes.

Kids don't come with instruction manuals, and parenting well doesn't just come naturally. Parents and other caregivers have to work on themselves, learn how to support child development, and gain positive skills that work well with kids. If you're going to have kids or work with kids, take a parenting class, read credible parenting sources, and hone a few mindfulness practices (believe me, you will need to woosah).

It's not some magical trick or any one thing you do to help your children behave. It's everything you do: all the pieces of the puzzle fitting together, working together, to set the course for happy, healthy, well-behaved kids. Again, set a firm foundation by being the best version of yourself, gaining parental knowledge, modeling how you want your kids to behave, and strengthening the parent-child relationship.

Build on that foundation by encouraging positive behavior and guiding positive choices through reinforcement strategies, such as praise, and by proactively setting up the environment for kids to behave. Honestly, that's most of the work! Inevitably, kids will misbehave. Have confidence in your skills to correct and discourage poor choices by using a nurturing but firm voice, by giving clear and consistent consequences, and by coaching your kids to choose better next time.

When you feel frustrated or angry with kids—because you will—breathe, step away, and take time to calm down before you respond or react. Understand that most kid misbehavior is not personal or intentional. Seek first to know the reason behind the behavior, and try to see the child's perspective in that moment (empathy). Kids make bad choices, but they are not "bad."

There are also no perfect parents. Give yourself a little grace, and keep trying to do the best you can. And finally, life is full of adversity. Give your child the gift of resilience so they can thrive through the good and bad times, by providing safe, stable, nurturing relationships and environments, and fill them with positive childhood experiences.

As I sign off, I have a final request.

Please use this book until it falls apart. Share it, and follow me on social media. Listen to my podcast—*KIDing Around with Dr. Candice*. Subscribe, rate, review, and like!

Website: www.drcandicemd.com
Facebook/Twitter/Instagram: @drcandicemd
YouTube: Candice W. Jones
Apple Podcast/SoundCloud/Google Play: *KIDing Around with Dr. Candice*
Electronic press kit: www.drcandicemd.com/media-kit

Bibliography

An adlerian resource book. North American Society of Adlerian Psychology. Accessed July 16, 2021. https://www.alfredadler.org

Andrade C, Radhakrishnan R. Prayer and healing: a medical and scientific perspective on randomized controlled trials. *Indian J Psychiatry.* 2009;51(4):247–253

APA resolution on physical discipline of children by parents. American Psychological Association. February 2019. Accessed June 18, 2021. https://www.apa.org/about/policy/resolution-physical-discipline.pdf

Bethell C, Jones J, Gombojav N, Linkenbach J, Sege R. Positive childhood experiences and adult mental and relational health in a statewide sample: associations across adverse childhood experiences levels. *JAMA Pediatr.* 2019;173(11):e193007

Global Initiative to End All Corporal Punishment of Children. November 2, 2017. Accessed June 18, 2021. https://endcorporalpunishment.org

Büssing A, Michalsen A, Khalsa SBS, Telles S, Sherman KJ. Effects of yoga on mental and physical health: a short summary of reviews. *Evid Based Complement Altern Med.* 2012;2012:165410

Chapman G, Campbell R. *The 5 Love Languages of Children.* Northfield Publishing; 2016

Cherry K. What is emotional intelligence? Verywell Mind. Updated June 3, 2020. Accessed July 16, 2021. https://www.verywellmind.com/what-is-emotional-intelligence-2795423

Choi SA, Hastings JF. Religion, spirituality, coping, and resilience among African Americans with diabetes. *J Relig Spiritual Soc Work.* 2019;38(1):93–114

Dweck CS. *Mindset: The New Psychology of Success.* Ballantine Books; 2016

Gershoff ET. *Report on Physical Punishment in the United States: What Research Tells Us About Its Effects on Children.* Center for Effective Discipline; 2008. Accessed June 18, 2021. http://www.nospank.net/gershoff.pdf

Gershoff ET. The research on spanking and its implications for intervention. American Psychological Association webinar. September 8, 2016. Accessed June 18, 2021. https://www.apa.org/act/resources/webinars/corporal-punishment-gershoff.pdf

Gershoff ET, Grogan-Kaylor A. Spanking and child outcomes: old controversies and new meta-analyses. *J Fam Psychol.* 2016;30(4):453–469. Accessed June 18, 2021. https://doi.org/10.1037/fam0000191

Ginsburg KR, Ginsburg I, Ginsburg T. *Raising Kids To Thrive: Balancing Love With Expectations and Protection With Trust.* American Academy of Pediatrics; 2015

Harris NB. *The Deepest Well: Healing Long-term Effects of Childhood Adversity.* Houghton Mifflin Harcourt Publishing Company; 2018

Horowitz JM, Graf N. Most U.S. teens see anxiety and depression as a major problem among their peers. February 20, 2019. Accessed July 16, 2021. https://www.pewresearch.org/social-trends/2019/02/20/most-u-s-teens-see-anxiety-and-depression-as-a-major-problem-among-their-peers

Koenig HG, George LK, Hays JC, Larson DB, Cohen HJ, Blazer DG. The relationship between religious activities and blood pressure in older adults. *Int J Psychiatry Med.* 1998;28(2):189–213

Latham GI. *The Power of Positive Parenting.* P & T Ink; 1994

Lavoie J, Leduc K, Arruda C, Crossman AM, Talwar V. Developmental profiles of children's spontaneous lie-telling behavior. *Cogn Dev.* 2017;41:33–45

Lisitsa E. An introduction to emotion coaching. June 8, 2012. Accessed June 18, 2021. https://www.gottman.com/blog/an-introduction-to-emotion-coaching

Luby JL, Barch D, Whalen D, Tillman R, Belden A. Association between early life adversity and risk for poor emotional and physical health in adolescence: a putative mechanistic neurodevelopmental pathway. *JAMA Pediatr.* 2017;171(12):1168–1175

Lucchetti G, Lucchetti ALG, Koenig HG. Impact of spirituality/religiosity on mortality: comparison with other health interventions. *Explore (NY)*. 2011;7(4):234–238

Masten AS. *Ordinary Magic: Resilience in Development*. Guilford Press; 2014

McLeod S. Piaget's theory and stages of cognitive development: background and key concepts of Piaget's theory. SimplyPsychology. Updated December 7, 2020. Accessed July 16, 2021. https://www.simplypsychology.org/piaget.html

Moullin S, Waldfogel J, Washbrook E. *Baby Bonds: Parenting, Attachment and a Secure Base for Children*. Sutton Trust; 2014. Accessed June 18, 2021. https://www.suttontrust.com/wp-content/uploads/2019/12/baby-bonds-final-1.pdf

Patton S. *Spare the Kids: Why Whupping Children Won't Save Black America*. Beacon Press; 2017

Sege RD, Siegel BS; American Academy of Pediatrics Council on Child Abuse and Neglect and Committee on Psychosocial Aspects of Child and Family Health. Effective discipline to raise healthy children. *Pediatrics*. 2018;142(6):e20183112

Traub F, Boynton-Jarrett R. Modifiable resilience factors to childhood adversity for clinical pediatric practice. *Pediatrics*. 2017;139(5):e20162569

What is positive discipline? Positive Discipline. Accessed July 16, 2021. https://www.positivediscipline.com/sites/default/files/what-is-positive-discipline.pdf

Who was BF Skinner? AppliedBehaviorAnalysisEDU.org. Accessed July 16, 2021. https://www.appliedbehavioranalysisedu.org/who-was-bf-skinner

Wolraich M, Felice ME, Drotar D. *The Classification of Child and Adolescent Mental Diagnoses in Primary Care: Diagnostic and Statistical Manual for Primary Care (DSM-PC)—Child and Adolescent Version*. American Academy of Pediatrics; 1996

Xu F, Bao X, Fu G, Talwar V, Lee K. Lying and truth-telling in children: from concept to action. *Child Dev*. 2010;81(2):581–596

Index